STRATHALDER
A HIGHLAND ESTATE

RODERICK GRANT

ISIS
LARGE PRINT
Oxford

First published in Great Britain 1978
by
Gordon and Cremonesi

Published in Large Print 2010 by ISIS Publishing Ltd.,
7 Centremead, Osney Mead, Oxford OX2 0ES
by arrangement with
Birlinn Ltd.

British Library Cataloguing in Publication Data
Grant, Roderick, 1941–
    Strathalder: a Highland estate. - - (Reminiscence)
    1. Highlands (Scotland) - - Social conditions - -
    20th century.
    2. Highlands (Scotland) - - Social life and
    customs - - 20th century.
    3. Highlands (Scotland) - - Description and travel.
    4. Large type books.
    I. Title II. Series
    941.1'5082–dc22

ISBN 978–0–7531–5241–6 (hb)
ISBN 978–0–7531–5242–3 (pb)

Printed and bound in Great Britain by
T. J. International Ltd., Padstow, Cornwall

For my mother and father

Introduction

You will not find Strathalder on any map of Scotland.
But, in reality, there are many examples of Strathalder
scattered throughout the countryside of the north-east
and the Highlands, in that region of the country
bounded and contained by the Grampian Mountains.
The Strathalder portrayed in this book is a typical
example of the country estate so much a distinctive
feature of Scottish rural life, as much a part of the
traditional heritage of the country as the blaze of
colourful tartan and the wild, haunting sound of the
bagpipes. Without the community formed by the
existence of an estate such as Strathalder even more
isolated and remote areas of Scotland would be
depopulated. The framework established by the
network of estates, each one with its laird, Scottish
counterpart of the English squire, has stood the test of
time and is still there today, diminished in size and
reduced in circumstances, perhaps, compared with
Victorian and Edwardian times; but alive and slowly
adapting to the changes demanded by a more complex
modern society.

I was born and raised on a Scottish country estate
where my father was a gamekeeper and my mother
tended our home set in the heart of woodland close to

1

the banks of a turbulent river. As a boy I was fortunate to have the freedom of thousands of acres in which to roam — wooded hillsides and moorland, open fields and the secret, often dangerous, gullies through which the river flowed. It was a life dominated by Nature — a world of foxes and rabbits, salmon and deer, red grouse and pheasants; a world where sight and talk of such creatures were a daily occurrence. In the course of my childhood I came into contact with many people from all walks of life; surprisingly, for such a remote place, far more than I could ever have expected to meet in a town; people such as the farm worker, the kitchen maid, the chauffeur, the laird himself and many of his guests, people with wealth beyond the bounds of my imagination at the time. To have been a child amid the community formed by a country estate was a unique experience because in such an environment it was possible to meet the widest cross-section of society, both wealthy and poor, idle and hard-working.

So, by the time I reached adulthood I had already met the invidious British class barrier head-on and found, because of this experience, that, quite simply, it did not exist as far as I was concerned; in other words, I simply refused to accept it. The estate had provided me with something that formal education had not — that people were people no matter their status in life or, for that matter, how much money they had in their pocket. In later life I also began to appreciate that living on a country estate as a child had, unwittingly, presented me with basic essentials which I would use in my novels and books — a love of wildlife and the countryside and an understanding and insight into the wide range of human character. Because, on an estate, you will find men and women of every shade of opinion and temperament. In this book I have tried to recapture the flavour of my own childhood memories linked to those of the men and women whose working lives have been spent in the service of an estate. I have deliberately chosen comparisons to be made between life as it is today and as it was in the 1920s, when the country estate had reached the height of its power and influence on the surrounding countryside.

Many people have helped by spending time both talking to me and in correspondence. I am most grateful to everyone for their generous assistance in helping me present a portrait of life on a typical Scottish country estate; an estate which I have called Strathalder and which, together with its inhabitants whose experiences are recorded in this book, is, in reality, an amalgam of all that is good and bad, both present and past, in countless similar establishments in rural districts across the face of Scotland.

Roderick Grant

CHAPTER
ONE

A rowan tree has its roots in the earth beneath the ruined floor; the branches spread out to interlock and brush the battered plaster on the walls, filling the space above where once the farmer's children slept; and in the gaping void no longer filled by timber and slates the crown of the tree drops like a shroud to touch the gables and the rough-hewn stones.

This was once a home, thirty distant years ago; a place where generations of men laughed and talked and swore at the wild, unbridled weather unleashed among them from the mountain within sight of the farm; where the women baked and cleaned, washed and ironed, scrubbed and polished, raised their children and, now and then, cried because of their poverty and at the hardship inflicted upon them all by wind and rain, frost and snow — and loneliness; and where the children, some sickly, some healthy, grew into adulthood, each affected in an individual way by the harshness of their surroundings so that when they went forth to a world beyond the strath they were marked by a particular spirit of independence riven deep inside them by the mere fact of having once existed in this most special place.

Like the house, most of the outbuildings, the cart sheds, the stables, the byre and the barn are now derelict. Only one has been kept in repair, the roof patched with sheets of corrugated iron, the door hanging on new hinges, even now within the space of months tainted by rust from the dampness in the air. In here the shepherd keeps his supply of dips, pesticides and insecticides, rolls of wire, fencing posts, nails, creosote — dozens of different items for a man with an infinite variety of jobs to do.

The days are long gone when, to be a shepherd, all a man needed was a crook, a good dog and an inner desire for solitude. Now, on an estate such as Strathalder, the shepherd is someone expected to lend a willing hand in all seasons — from spying on the intruding vermin, foxes, hooded crows and other predators, on the grouse moor and reporting their whereabouts to the head gamekeeper situated amid the tightly-knit estate complex on the lower ground far down in the valley, to repairing boundary fences and keeping the hill roads in a decent state of repair.

The hand of change has touched him as it has touched so many people who live and work on Strathalder, made them adapt, willingly and unwillingly, to a new way of life; perhaps, for some, less arduous physically, but for most, more complex and bringing with it new problems and stresses unknown to their forebears who saw the estate as their shield against the vagaries of the outside world. This is no longer possible for the inhabitants of Strathalder. The estate may still, directly or indirectly, provide a number of them with a livelihood but it cannot protect and nurture them as once it did. It is no longer inviolate itself from the outside pressures of a modern and, at times, hostile world; the laird is no longer the omnipotent figure as was his father, or his grandfather in a dim, though golden, past. In a modern society, fraught with a bewildering preponderance of technology and ruthless economics, everyone — worker and laird — has had to adapt in order to survive. There have been victims; those families forced to leave the strath because work was no longer available, those approaching retirement age who might, in better times, have expected a rent-free house in which to live for the remainder of their days, but who now have to compete on disadvantageous terms with outsiders for the purchase of a country cottage.

Were this farmhouse, with its rowan tree among its foundations and its moss and lichens clinging to crumbling walls, in some more accessible place, then even its skeleton might have been brought back to life again as has been the case with so many others close to the roads down in the valley. But up here there is no road, except for a muddy track threading its way for several miles through the moorland from a bridge beside the waterfall on the river. And so it has been left in peace, an empty shell through which the sighing wind ripples and where, on a summer's day, the silence has a penetrating quality, broken only by the screeching of lapwings nesting in a marshy field beyond the sheep fanks and the more distant, melancholy cries of the curlews, like a lament for the souls long since departed from the moor.

Laughter and tears, sorrow and joy have all touched the lives of those who once lived on this isolated upland farm. Moments of happiness when outlying neighbours trudged to the house to celebrate a birth or to drink a toast to a daughter or son about to be married; dark times of tragedy when, in 1917, the mud-filled trenches of Passchendaele claimed a son whose craving for adventure led him to volunteer to fight with the army, and later a father of seven who died when his tractor went out of control on the steep, final descent of the track, man and machine bursting through the frail, wooden parapet of the bridge and plunging into the swollen river where it boiled at the foot of the waterfall. They recovered the tractor. It took two days to lift it from the bed of the river. It took a week to locate the farmer's body; only a matter of minutes to recover it from its resting place.

But the widow and her seven children, despite two sons having reached adulthood and fully capable of running the farm, could no longer stay in the place. There was only one way by which to reach the farm and this was across the wooden bridge. Every step on the creaking, weather-worn timbers was, so she said, like walking across her husband's grave. So they deserted what had been their home for two decades. And when they left no one came to take their place. After a couple of years the roof was removed from the farmhouse and house and outbuildings became a mere sheltering place for sheep and estate workers caught on the moor by a sudden storm. The rowan trees took over and grew unchecked. Birds nested in the chimneys, wasps in crevices in the walls. For several years, until she was spotted by a vigilant shepherd, a vixen reared her litters of cubs beneath the foundations of the washhouse. In the space of one more decade a wilderness was firmly established among what had once been relative neatness and order.

The farm is not alone. On Strathalder it has many counterparts, pockets of neglect and decay here and there throughout a seemingly endless expanse of moorland. It is as if the moor has been left to the ghosts and the grouse and the transient sheep. Human life has retreated to the softer belly of the strath and although the uplands have not been totally abandoned they are no longer a place of habitation; just a part of the estate to be visited from time to time, by the laird and members of his family and guests to shoot the grouse, perhaps to fish in the river when the salmon are running fresh in from the sea or, in more leisurely fashion to entice the brown trout lurking in the peaty darkness of one of the numerous hill lochs. The shepherd, the gamekeeper and the deer stalker come here too, each with his individual task to perform, but each with a degree of interest in the other's particular duty, linked as they are to the prime necessity of ensuring the smooth running of all aspects of the estate. Now, perhaps even more than at any time, it is important that the various departments within the estate co-operate and harmonize in a common aim; that of maintaining the good management of a business on which everyone depends for the security of their future existence. Gone are the days of empires within an empire. In industry and commerce they would talk of rationalization. On Strathalder, grudgingly accepted or enthusiastically praised, this pruning and reshaping of a traditional way of life is merely described as "changing with the times".

And the "times" they speak of have been good and bad. They will continue to be so. There is nothing new in their having "to change with the times". An estate such as Strathalder has been adapting and adjusting since the zenith of its powers at the end of the First World War. But it took two world wars and a succession of governments to bring about a confrontation with the stark realities of change, some in recent years having to be accomplished in months rather than years. For a time events moved more swiftly than owner, employee and tenant farmer would have wished as they were all carried along on a relentless tide of circumstance.

It is more settled now in this streamlined Strathalder. In a way, for many of the older inhabitants, life could be described as being more akin to what it was like in the time of their forebears. There is, once again, a degree of continuity. And on an estate this, above all else, is what is welcomed and cherished by everyone; continuity of purpose, continuity of a familiar pattern where life can go on undisturbed, yet (and perhaps to many, this is the most important factor of all, now as in the past) where there can always be an open respect between the laird, as employer, and those whose livelihood is dependent upon his survival. The benevolent laird may have gone, become an anachronism, but his modern counterpart must never forget that, although his estate may, to him, be both home and business, the true success of his enterprise depends on his rapport with the inhabitants of the boundless acres he controls.

Running an estate has been likened to operating a ship. Keep the crew informed and happy and all will proceed smoothly. Fail to do this and the first seeds of discontent have been sown. It is an apt analogy. Few who have forgotten or ignored it have prospered; not so much in material terms, but as inheritors of the tradition of service and loyalty which are the hallmarks of those born into the pattern of estate work. Because it is, quite simply, a way of life for many; a job which continues within a family for generation after generation, making the worker every bit as much of a traditionalist as the laird. It is a way of life which survives despite the modern pressures put upon it.

The derelict farmhouses and cottages scattered around the moors where rowan and birch run rampant among the ruins are reminders of a more glorious age; signposts to the past.

Look to the valley; to the wooded slopes either side of the river, to the fields where sleek, fat cattle graze contentedly and where when the plough turns over the earth it emerges as rich, dark loam. The mansion house nestles among the trees close to a bend in the river, the village no more than a mile away. This is the hub of Strathalder estate; the central point around which revolves the life and work of the community. For generations it has always been this way; only now, the axis is narrower as if the inhabitants have grown tired of fighting the elements on the distant boundaries high on the uplands and retreated to the shelter of a more gentle landscape.

And on the hillsides beneath the mountain are the monuments to their departure; the shells of buildings, the piles of stone, the wind-flayed trees rising unhindered from the silent rubble of another age.

CHAPTER
TWO

Depopulation of the Scottish countryside is a feature of life the people have lived with for many years now. Indeed, some would say that the Scots have faced it for far too long. Of course it is not a predicament faced solely by the Scots; in England, as in other countries too, the drift from the land has gone on unchecked because in towns and cities there are jobs and money and in the rural districts both are often items in short supply. In Scotland, however, particularly in the north, it has been, and still is to some extent, a problem of greater magnitude. The Scottish climate can be a harsh one, especially in the winter months and as so much country work, indeed the bulk of estate employment is in outdoor jobs, it seems logical for people to seek the relatively well-paid and more comfortable work to be found in the towns. Helping to hasten the exodus from the countryside has been a collection of motley and varying factors; the increased use of machinery on farms, the closure of rural schools and on estates the vast reduction of the labour force because economics do not allow the modern laird to indulge himself by maintaining a massive work force on what, nowadays, would be regarded by many as the pure pursuit of pleasure. The laird may be wealthier than those who surround him, but no longer is he the man of abundant wealth which, most likely, was the position enjoyed by his immediate ancestors.

With this change in everyone's circumstances so, too, has the social pattern of estate life and the relationship between worker and laird been transformed. It has not, however, changed out of all recognition with the past; traces of it are still in evidence both as regards the estate itself and in the attitude of the older members of the work force towards the laird himself. To them, because he has a special position in being the landowner, he is still the object of particular distinction and respect. He is their link with the past. But for many of the younger employees, some of whom came to the area merely in order to seek work, there is, of course, no individual attachment either to the laird as their employer or to the past as the others knew it. To them, the most important factor in their lives is to have a job at all in a region of high unemployment, whether in town or country.

To people like Donald Watson, retired now and living in a house in the village, Strathalder estate has always been a special place. He knew it as a youth in the 1920s and he looks at it today with a mixture of pleasant memories and regret at the passing of an era which saw Strathalder as giving life to this isolated community of country people. In many ways Strathalder was his life.

In the 1920s this estate was a very close-knit community, not just in the general aims of laird and employees, but even down to the siting of the houses and offices. The heart of the estate where the mansion house — or as we estate folk always call it, the Big House — stood, with a short distance away a cluster of employees' houses, was in many ways exactly like a small village.

The Big House was entirely enclosed by trees and rhododendron bushes, varieties of all kinds, large and small. In the spring the blooms were magnificent, reds and blues, pinks and whites, all shades and all sizes, the most splendid having great scarlet flowers covered with black flecks and spots. There were kinds you never see nowadays in any garden, anywhere; only in the grounds of old estates such as this. So, these bushes and the trees, beech and pine, some oak, a few fir and spruce, provided seclusion for the occupants of the Big House.

In close proximity there was what was known as the stable yard, which had become a collection of houses for the gardeners and certain members of the household staff. Then a little further away on an outer fringe were the houses and accommodation for the remaining workers, foresters, farm labourers, some of the gamekeepers, the bothies where the single men lived. Around this area was situated a variety of buildings housing the blacksmith's shop, the joiners' and carpenters' workshop, the store with the timber. The estate also kept two stonemasons on the staff at that time. Their yard was here, close to the estate office and forestry headquarters, the yard for carts and equipment.

Right in the middle of this community was an excellent recreation hall, built of Canadian cedar shingles and that consisted of a billiard room, reading room with dance floor, concert hall, everything. There was no wireless or television then so all entertainment was devised and performed on the estate. Occasionally, a film would be brought in and shown, but this only happened now and again. For the most part the estate people arranged their own activities. There was also a church where services were held once a month, with the minister coming up from the town to take the service; a primary school, with around forty pupils and two teachers (it was an Education Board school, but a great number of the pupils were estate workers' children) and a lovely nine-hole golf course for use by the laird and his family and guests as well as the employees. The church is still there, of course, but the golf course was put under the plough years ago. The school closed down recently due, really, to lack of pupils. There were more young couples with children living on estates in my young days than there are now so, of course, this provided the school with plenty of pupils.

There was certainly a distinction between the laird and the ordinary working people, but somehow or other he had a more direct contact with the estate people and their needs seemed to be looked after far better than they are now. The laird was always looked upon as somebody of quite some stature and deeply respected by people of all ages. There was no fear on the part of the worker. There was never any fear of losing your house or your job, providing you did your work. But he would find out if there were any problems or worries, or any family troubles, and do what he could to help. The whole estate was run on a very, very friendly basis. Of course he was there, resident on the estate, practically all the time. There was no question of having an absentee landlord as so often is the case nowadays. He probably spent nine months of each year living in the Big House and the remainder of the time in the south — in Edinburgh or in London. But this was his home.

He lived and entertained like a true laird, a proper country gentleman. He was a very wealthy man and he had his butler, two footmen, pantry boy, cook, about four kitchen staff, a housekeeper, six housemaids, a handyman, two chauffeurs. The house was filled with people with some job or other to do. The difference is that now part of the house has been pulled down in order to turn it into a smaller, more easily maintained mansion, and two wives of estate workers do all the cleaning and are only required to cook in the case of there being any special guests to be entertained.

In the 1920s everything was laid on. We had our own dairy which supplied the workers with milk at one penny a pint. Potatoes — we could have as many as we liked for nothing. Everybody kept hens, so there were plenty of eggs to eat and the houses all had good gardens at the back for cultivating vegetables and growing fruit bushes — blackcurrants, red and white currants, gooseberries and raspberries. Although the wages were small it really was a happy, contented life, certainly for someone like myself, a fit, strong, young unmarried man. Living in a bothy I received coal and firewood, paraffin for the lamps (there was no electricity laid on as far as the estate in those days) and although my first wages were only around twenty-five shillings a week I managed to cope remarkably well — and still save some money. Some might think it a very enclosed simple way of life. Well, it was simple, I suppose, if that means being free of all the niggling pressures one comes up against nowadays in even the most remote spot. It seems impossible now to shut out the outside world no matter where you live. In those days

18

for most of us there was no outside world. Our world was here. We all felt that the estate really cared for us as workers, that our services, no matter how menial, were appreciated. And this spirit of goodwill engendered by the laird really did create the best possible atmosphere in which to live and work. I can't recall any friction, any jealousy or spiteful gossip among the estate workers and their families then. This seems to be a modern phenomenon. It has crept in everywhere, no matter which estate you go to.

As estates have shrunk in size and adapted to modern commercial methods, discontentment has appeared and grown worse, just as it has done in almost every walk of life you can think of in society today. Lots of things are responsible for this state of affairs on estates — mechanization, say, on the farms, on the hills, in the forests, has meant a decrease in staff. For example, in the game department, when I was a young man and first knew the estate, there was the head gamekeeper, ten under-keepers and two ponymen. Now it has shrunk to one head keeper and five under-keepers who spend all the fishing season on the river looking after paying guests. As a result their beats are neglected so that the vermin are able to run riot. Once certain types of vermin, stoats, weasels, foxes and the like, get a hold then it's a full-time job just to keep them down, far less get rid of them.

Some of this friction also comes about due to the way factors now administer the estates on behalf of the lairds. Just as in every other aspect of estate life where there are good workers and bad workers so, too, are there good factors and bad ones. It always has been like this. And when you've got a good one, a man who knows every single thing about the place as well, if not better, than the owner himself, then all goes smoothly. The responsible factor will always consult with the heads of the various departments and never interfere with the day-to-day running of the estate. He'll leave the individual bosses to get on with that and take what decisions have to be made about administration in consultation with them.

Now, in the old days the factor was the overseer of all the departments, but there was a definite delegation of authority to each head of department. To the rank and file in, say, the game department, the farm department or the forestry department, any queries any man had were simply with the head of that particular department. So if you were a lesser mortal, the factor meant nothing to you. He was somebody important, but he had nothing to do directly with you.

Unfortunately, nowadays — and this is a thing that has crept in gradually in recent years — the factor on most estates has taken over more and more authority to himself, more or less undermining the power of the departmental heads. That, in itself, is against harmony. I mean, it's no longer a fact that if you've committed any misdemeanour then your department head will deal with it. Most likely the factor will step in and very often it ends up with two disgruntled people, the worker and the head of department. And if the worker is the man who feels most aggrieved then naturally he's going to complain to his colleagues about it. No doubt their reactions will be mixed. Some will side with him, while others will favour the head of department. Just the right ingredients for a simmering row.

Part of the trouble is that very often I think the modern factor takes on too much so that with so much work to do individual items are neglected. It only needs a few vital things to be forgotten about by him in the course of a busy period or, perhaps, what seems like too long a time being taken by him to reach an important decision, for discontent to break out. You see, quite naturally if you're a head of department and you find the factor constantly interfering in what you rightly believe to be your sole concern, you'll only stand for it for so long and either have a row about it or say, well if he's going to stick his nose in where it's not wanted, let him do it. This, quite often, is the start of trouble for all concerned. This sort of behaviour invariably leads to friction of the worst kind.

An estate can count itself lucky now if it manages to attract young fellows to work for it. Many of the young men — and women too — tend to drift away from the rural districts after they leave school in search of what they regard as better paid and more interesting jobs in the towns and cities. And up here in the north of Scotland they don't have to go very far nowadays. At one time they went south, to Glasgow or Edinburgh, even to London in search of employment. But now, with North Sea oil exploration and development growing steadily, becoming bigger and more prosperous all the time, they can often find work nearer home because so many new industries have sprung up as a result of the oil boom in this area.

Personally, I think that television has not been the best of influences in the country districts. It creates discontent. It makes people want to get away to the brighter lights to see some of the life which they see every night on the screen. In a way you can't blame them, I suppose. But the lack of young people willing to stay on and work locally, most probably on the estate, has made a tremendous difference to the entire neighbourhood. The estate tends to have an ageing work force nowadays, depleted as it might be compared to former years. This change in the whole pattern of country life you can see all around you. Not only here, but in almost any rural community.

Wherever you go on this estate you'll see houses that have been sold off and are now being used purely as summer houses, holiday homes, occupied perhaps for only a couple of months in the year. You look back and you think of the families once raised in these houses and of how they're now scattered to all corners of the world. It makes you sad to think of all these people gone from their birth-place. Even worse, to my mind, are the number of houses in total ruins. Within my lifetime I've seen them occupied, then when the last family left they were just allowed to decay and eventually crumble to the ground all together. This is very sad to see.

I knew these houses, was inside many of them when they were inhabited. I saw the fires lit and the curtains drawn on a wild winter's night. I saw the children growing up — many of them growing up alongside me at the same school — and I shared in the family fun. Quite often I'd be a visitor to take part in celebrations — perhaps at Christmas or New Year, on somebody's birthday; special times when, poor though the family might be, an extra effort was made to get some enjoyment out of the occasion. Now, I go along the road and I see these places just heaps of stone and rubble, the gardens choked with nettles and grass, weeds of all kinds. Saddest of all is to see in the middle of this wilderness an overgrown fruit bush and to remember the days when, as a youngster, I'd helped to pick the fruit, spurred on by the promise of a slice of pie or bread and jam from the woman of the house.

22

Sometimes I stop and lean on the wall and remember. It's probably the worst thing I could do. Because all that was in the past. It can never be recaptured again. The memory of it is there, as vivid as ever. But it's a poor substitute for the real thing. I'd really like to see the houses lived in, preferably by people employed in the district, on the estate, on the farms, just as they once were. It may be very peaceful here with so few people around, but it's an uneasy peace. The district has been emptied of people, the people whose roots were once firmly planted here. In return we have the incomers. Many of them are no more than mere nomads — here for a few days, then gone again. What they get out of it beats me. All I know is that they bring precious little into the place. Some of them do try to involve themselves, but only a few. For the most part they keep to themselves. They lead their lives and we, those of us who are still around, lead ours.

So, the population has been drastically cut down, wages have certainly gone up, but many of the amenities once enjoyed by the estate worker have vanished. Things like free potatoes, vegetables and milk. Everything has now either got to be grown — or bought. The standard of living is now really much lower than it was in the period, say, from around 1927 to 1932. At that time the average farm worker would have been earning around £2 to £2.10s a week whereas today he'll be getting in the region of £35 to £40. But he'll be a lot worse off today because out of his take-home pay every single thing will have to be paid for at today's vastly inflated prices. So if he's got to pay for the basic essentials he was once entitled to receive as part of his job it's little wonder he is forced to go further afield in order to get as much money as he can possibly earn.

Another problem is transport. In the old days everyone had bicycles. It used to mean quite a thing to a person to get a decent bicycle. To be able to afford it. It was quite a status symbol. But you find now that there's few young people without either a motor cycle or a car. And half the time they are people who can't afford it. Either to buy the thing or to run it. So that has cut down their standard of living. People have become lazy. They'll never think about cycling anywhere now. They must have motorised transport. It's regarded as essential, but often it's just an excuse to keep up with the others around you. Of course, for those who don't own cars and live in the more remote rural areas the problems are quite acute. If you live off a main bus route then the difficulties are enormous. You are in trouble. In this part of the world it is only the main roads that are serviced by buses. Local shops have closed down and whereas at one time, up to just a year or two ago, the country districts were all served by visiting vans — general grocer, butcher and fishmonger, a baker even — these are now definitely in a minority. It has become too expensive, both in wages and petrol, for shopkeepers to provide such services. And who are we to blame them?

No, the countryside has become impoverished in many ways. We had a railway not far from here at one time. In addition there were two bus services in opposition to each other. The services were good. The fares were kept down by virtue of the competition. When the axe fell on the railway we were promised there would be an increased bus service to compensate for the loss. What really happened was that the small bus company was taken over by the large one, the services worsened and instead of the progress we were asked to accept, or which more truthfully was forced on us, we have ended up much worse off than we were many years ago. This estate was much more accessible and easy to travel to and from by the working man and his family in the 1920s than it is today.

The Second World War and also National Service were responsible for the decline in the number of young men willing to do estate work. The young folk got out into the world, they saw how the rest of the world lived. They got their first taste of real money. I suppose that being human the more they got, the more they wanted. This drove away a great number of young people, the country people, who would, if they had stayed, have had the knowledge to follow in their fathers' footsteps. They were coaxed away. They might have gone to Glasgow to the shipyards on the Clyde, to Corby to the steelworks there, or to Aberdeen to work in a factory. And the vacuum left by their departure was either not filled, or filled by people who were rejects from the very society our own youngsters were joining; the dregs from any town employment. This is where the rot began to show itself, the time when it really set in with a vengeance. Once people had got a taste of life in the outside world, away from the sheltered existence of the estate, they became easily disgruntled if they were forced, through circumstances, family affairs, this sort of thing, to return. Of course, many of them never did return. And in the long run I doubt very much if they were any better off. Oh yes, they might have had a bit more money in their pockets, a modern home, but from what I got to hear about some of them, they never seemed to be able to settle down. They were always on the move. They became restless people. You see, by leaving here, uprooting themselves, severing their links with the estate, they had lost one of the basic features of life amid such surroundings as you find on an estate like this; true beauty and a wonderful sense of calm.

The average laird nowadays is also a very different person from the type who was around in the 1930s and 1930s. The modern laird is fully occupied with the running of his estate. It is probably the sole source of his income. If so, then he wants to get every possible penny out of the place. He will not merely be supervising, but taking an active part in the work. Quite a number of the new lairds, the sons and grandsons of previous lairds who have inherited their property, work on the estate alongside their employees. This is a new style of life for them. And they seem to enjoy it. They will roll up their shirt sleeves and work in the forestry department, the game department and on the Home Farm. Now, they are probably considered by many of the work force to be utter nuisances, but believe me, the ones I know do as much work in a day as any of their employees. The lairds have been forced into this acceptance of a working role, whereas before they were merely country gentlemen living on inherited income and never for a moment dirtying their hands. But now, they simply have to set to and help out. They work quite happily alongside their men. Everything has got to be channelled into making money to cover the increased costs of labour, materials, every single thing that goes into the running of an estate.

The whole outlook is different. The laird is no longer placed on a pedestal like he used to be. I think the word feudal is the wrong one to describe the relationship between laird and employee in the past. It was a form of respect. A mutual respect. This is not given now. You can hear employees talking to the laird nowadays and being practically impudent. The younger generation think nothing of it. And it is accepted by the laird. He has to. He knows he has to tread warily or else he'll lose workers faster than he could ever replace them. It is the hardest job in the world to find good people to work on the estate. So, if the laird has got himself a good craftsman, a man who works hard although he might be inclined to shoot his mouth off a little, then he has got to look after that man if he wants to keep him. The price he is forced to pay is this new trait of familiarity.

I prefer the past. There is absolutely no doubt about this. I am quite certain in my mind that the past was better. I think when respect was given to the laird and his family the estate was a very happy community. It was a good place in which to work and live. Now that everything is on a more familiar and easy-going basis it's very much a case all the time of "dog bites dog". Everyone is vying with each other for the friendship of the laird. And at times it's no holds barred. Probably the best way to describe this state of affairs is to say that there is a great deal of fawning and crawling going on now. In the old days the laird would be polite, yet aloof. It didn't matter who you were, there was just no possibility of one employee gaining more favour than any other. But now, there's a lot of competition among employees to get on special terms with the laird. Quite a cut-throat business. And so stupid. The funny thing is that it's all come about because today everyone is supposed to be equal. Rubbish. In the old days there was really more equality than there is now. There was certainly a clear, distinct barrier between the laird and the workers, but you probably found there was a much closer and more genuine contact. The old laird was never condescending. He would know every detail of what was happening to the different families on his estate. And his interest was genuine. Sincere. Absolutely natural and accepted by all.

There's a great deal of suspicion now if the laird takes a particular interest in any one family. If he's seen going into a worker's house others will be asking, "Why is he going there?" There will be resentment that this worker may be going to be favoured or that perhaps the laird is hearing of things he shouldn't know anything about concerning other workers. It's all very petty. But then many of the grumbles and grievances people have in life today are petty and trifling. Estate folk are no different.

But when you've known the past and you've seen just how much harmony there once was, it makes you dispirited. Not only for the present — but for the future.

CHAPTER
THREE

Strathalder's home farm — the base from which all the estate's farms are administered — is a cluster of buildings sheltered by spruce trees in a hollow a mile or so from the mansion house. In winter the track from the road to the farm is no longer pitted with pot-holes and awash with mud as it was in the years between the two world wars; the surface is tarred now and when the men arrive for work the majority are in their own cars, some of the younger ones astride powerful motor cycles.

The young ones are in the minority now, for no longer is there the same urge to leave school and work on the land when higher wages and more comfortable conditions can be obtained further afield in town and city. There is, of course, less work to be done by hand, requiring fewer people to do it, because like so many other features of modern life estate farming has become highly mechanized and sophisticated.

Agriculture has always been a prominent feature at Strathalder. Indeed, any Scottish estate will have relied, in one form or another, on an income from its farms. Until the end of the Second World War most estate farms were let to tenant farmers, the estate receiving a rent and in the usual way, as landlord, being responsible for major improvements to the land and buildings. This continued on a decreasing scale throughout the 1950s and into the 1960s. As each tenancy came to an end the estate took over the farm until, at the present time, most are now controlled by what is called the estate's Agricultural Department, the entire operation under the supervision of a farm manager.

On Strathalder farms no longer compete. A few concentrate on cereal growing and crops such as potatoes and turnips, another has a pig unit, where methods of intensive rearing and fattening are used to ensure maximum production, several are reserved for the fattening of beef cattle. There is also a small dairy herd, a poultry unit where the emphasis is on birds for the frozen chicken market and close to the moorland, with its opportunities for summer grazing, is the sheep farm. When agriculture is organized and administered on such a scale it is a highly complex and cost-effective business. Gone are the days of patchwork farming and of a vast army of men performing an infinite variety of tasks, many of which were no more than sheer drudgery from dawn to dusk, no matter the time of year.

The average farm worker, while being paid more adequately than his pre-war counterpart, is still well behind the recognized industrial wage on his basic rates of pay, although his craftsmanship is now rewarded by additional payments and there are scales of promotion to which he can now rise. No longer is the farm worker on an estate considered to be the poor relation in terms of skills. There was a time when to work on a farm earned the employee the title of farm labourer. The heavy, often difficult and dirty tasks are still there to be done, but much of the labour has been removed from them due to the use of machines. When fields are drained an excavator and driver handle the job which once it would have taken a gang of men to do, digging the trenches in rain and mud for days on end. Harvests can be gathered with combine harvesters, potatoes lifted from the soil by a machine, the ploughing in winter and spring accomplished in weeks by tractor or deep mechanical plough when once it would have taken teams of horsemen the full span of the appropriate months to complete the operation.

All the same, farm work is and always has been a job for the man who can withstand the rigours of the climate, in particular the Scottish weather, when the winter months can be long and hard, alternating between rain and snow and sleet, and in the summer speed is necessary to take advantage of the good days for the harvesting and storing of the season's crops.

Bill Morrison has seen all aspects of farming life and work, from the days when Strathalder was landlord to a host of farms scattered throughout the estate, to the present situation when so much is controlled by so few. He welcomes many of the changes, in particular those that have meant a reduction in the general conditions of hardship suffered by farm workers for far too long. But when he reflects on a lifetime spent on the land he now sees little evidence of pride in the attitude of the estate farm worker towards his job. In his day, he maintains, they had poverty, but somehow they usually managed to produce an abundance of pride.

My father was a farm worker getting paid £5 to £6 every six months when he was a young man in the 1870s–1880s. I was born in 1900. I remember as a youngster — oh, I'd have been about ten at the time — he was earning £17 for the whole year with meal, milk and potatoes thrown in. And he was there on the same farm for fourteen years and he was only making £18 a year at the end of that time. All that work, hard work from early morning to night, and he'd only earned for himself a rise in wages of £1 a year. He left that job to go back to his old home territory, where he'd been born and brought up, for 1s.6d a week more.

For his £18 a year he was cattleman and farm grieve — an overseer or foreman if you like — doing a ten-hour day, starting at six o'clock in the morning. Of course, he would have been up out of bed a good bit before this to get his breakfast and then off to work to get there in good time to start. In those days farmers were tyrants when it came to their men keeping time — they made few allowances for those chaps who persisted in turning up late. As well as making sure he was there in the farmyard for work at six o'clock one of his jobs as grieve was to be out and about among the other cottages around the farm to make certain the men were ready for their work at six. Oh aye, they speak about folks nowadays watching the clock, but even then, in the heart of the countryside, the ticking of the clock and the hands of time ruled and dominated the life of the ordinary working man. He

33

could keep a job — or lose it — by the amount of attention he paid to the hands of the clock.

He had sixty head of cattle and half a dozen young horses and he had to see to it that they were put out to graze and brought in every day. And in the winter he had to make sure that enough turnips were pulled for that sixty head of cattle to eat — one of the worst jobs on a farm in the winter months when every day up here in these parts the frost can lie thick on the leaves and turn the ground rigid, like rock. All this was done by hand. There were no machines for lifting and chopping like they have now. And if the weather was really bad, making it impossible for any work to be done outdoors, there was always a job to be found inside for the men, say in the barn, dressing corn. I know there were places where if the weather was bad it meant no work at all and no pay. God, that really was an inhuman practice, when a man's ability to feed himself and his family was dictated by the weather; when, during the winter in particular, a man would look up at the sky each morning he awoke and feel his heart sinking when he saw the storm clouds gathering over the hills, then feel the rain — or worse still the snow — on his face as he walked from his cottage to the farm and he knew deep down that there would be no work done that day and he'd be spending it in idleness and be even poorer as a result of it.

But on his farm and on mine this never happened, thank the Lord. Rain, hail or shine you got your money — and you always had some sort of job to do. The farmer made damn sure of that. He wanted his money's-worth.

I started work on a farm in January, 1914. I left school at the end of the month and I earned £1 from that time up to the end of May. Four months' working for £1. For that I was just the lad about the farm, a general dog'sbody at everyone's beck and call. I had the milking cows to sort out, clean the byres, put in fresh straw, feed them. And the wee calves — I had to look after them. I enjoyed doing that. They were devils some of them, always charging about the place when your back was turned. Then I was hired again for the summer and for the next six months I earned £5.

I had to take the milking cows in every day, including Sundays — at seven o'clock in the morning in the summer. I had to herd them in from the fields and at eight o'clock after the milking was finished I had to drive them out to the fields again, back to the grazing. Then I had to take them in again at mid-day (they were milked three times a day) and I daren't put them out again until about three in the afternoon because it was too hot for them out in the open. I then had to have them back inside at seven o'clock in the evening for another milking at eight. Then near to nine o'clock when this was done I was driving them out to the fields again so that they could graze overnight. Back and fore all bloody day, day in and day out. Lord, the cows got to know me so well and the regular habits I had that each time I appeared at the field gate they'd raise their heads, look at me, then the first ones would make their way over in my direction and hopefully the rest would just follow without any bother. There was always an awkward customer but she was usually rounded-up quite quickly by the dog or by both of us while the others milled about in the gateway waiting to plod back to the farm.

For the whole of that six months I had no time off. I was working every day, seven days a week, doing the same damned thing. Mind you, even if I had been able to get time off I doubt if I could have gone very far from the farm. I lived-in there (I was quite a distance away from where my parents lived) and as we only got paid at the end of a six-month term (at the end of May or the end of November) I had no money in my pocket to pay for any enjoyment whatsoever. Sheer, bloody slave labour — that's what it was. But you know at the time, as a youngster, I never thought overmuch about the hard work and conditions of service. It was just that the monotony of having to drive the cows in and out, back and fore, every day, began to get on my nerves. So I decided that when my six months were up I would seek a job on another farm. True, I'd get more money — or so I hoped — but mainly I would try to get something to do which would give me some variety.

On this farm, my first, I lived on the place as I've said, and was fed by the farmer's wife. She was no great hand as a cook and had little imagination but then, as a young lad, I had no great knowledge myself of different kinds of food. So I ate what she put in front of me and never complained. You had your brose (boiling milk on oatmeal) in the morning, then about 11.30a.m. or 12.00, mashed potatoes, potato soup or stoved potatoes with always a basin of milk on the table and plates of newly-baked oatcakes, plenty of them. Then at six o'clock at night you'd go in and get a plate of porridge and a cup of tea. That was all. And, of course, I still had work to do after this seeing to those bloody cows. We just had to eat it and say nothing. It was a pretty bare diet — and monotonous. Just like the job I was doing.

So, at the end of the term in November I was up and off. I'd had enough of that job and of course with the Great War just started you could always get more money by going to a new place than you'd have got staying on in the old job. I was on top of the world when I was offered £10 and the chance of being taught how to use a plough. I thought — this is it. I'm really going to get somewhere here. I thought it a vast sum of money — a great fee as we always called the money offered to hire us.

However, no sooner did I get to this new farm than the grieve who had engaged me on behalf of the farmer decided to leave straightaway. You see, he'd been bribed by the farmer to engage two men and if he got them cheaply enough then he, the grieve, could have a rise in his own wages. So the grieve got hold of two young lads, myself and another chap, and though I was fair pleased with my £10 he really had got us very cheap considering all the work we were expected to do. But then the farmer double-crossed him. He wouldn't give him his promised rise. At once he told the farmer in no uncertain manner what he thought of him and left on the spot. This was on a Friday morning. I remember the farmer coming into the stable with a glowering face. He was shaking all over, barely able to control his rage. He spoke to the other lad first, told him the grieve had left and said to him to get a pair of horses out and get on with some ploughing. But the other chap says to him, "The grieve's leaving, is he?"

"Oh aye, he's leaving," says the farmer. "I'm well rid of him."

"Well," says the other chap, "he engaged me and he seems a fair enough bloke to me so I'm leaving along with him."

"Oh well, please yourself," says the farmer. "You'll make a fine pair."

So he then came to me at the back of the stable and without any explanation just ordered me out to one of the fields to pull turnips. But I'd heard everything that had been said and by now he had a wild sort of look about him. I thought to myself that he'd have me doing my own job along with those jobs the other two should have been doing and that he'd let this situation run for as long as he possibly could. So for the first time in my life I stood up to a boss and I told him,

"Oh, I'm not going to pull any turnips. Not bloody likely. If they're both leaving, then I'm going too."

You know, I thought he'd strike me. He was a big man, in his fifties, used to ordering folks about the place. And here was me, a raw youngster of fifteen answering him back. I saw his fists clenching at his sides, but he just stared at me with two eyes full of scorn and says,

"Oh well, you can try it. But you'll not find it easy to get another job on a farm around here. I'll see to that."

"I'll chance it," I said. And at that he turned on his heels and walked out of the stable.

I left that very morning, the grieve and the other lad helping to carry my trunk, with what few possessions I had packed inside it. The farmer and his wife were in the yard when I went past them. They turned their backs and went inside. I heard the door slam shut. As we all had a laugh at their bad temper I imagined the pair of them rowing with each other. They were that sort of folk — the kind who fight when the odds are against them. It was a good move to have made on my part. Oh yes, I'd taken a gamble, but luck was on my side. A week later I was hired by another farmer and got £6 more — £16 instead of £10.

There were all sorts of farmers, good ones and bad. Some could be kind-hearted and generous and both themselves and their wives took a real interest in the workers and their families. Most of the farms were rented from the estate — tenant farmers they were called. A few were owned by the farmers themselves. Very few, really, at the time I'm speaking about — the end of the Great War and on from there. One or two of the owner-occupier farmers liked to think of themselves as a cut above the rest — gentleman farmers. But no one took much notice of their airs and graces. On an estate, especially in those days, most of the people working in all manner of jobs were the descendants of the previous generation of workers. So everybody knew how this one or that one had come to inherit the farm and how they had made their money. And, I can tell you, there were a few real rogues among them.

They made a good killing out of food production during the war years and when it was over some of them even had the nerve to plead poverty when it came to a workman haggling for an extra few pounds on his wages for a term's work. But we knew the rogues and we laughed at them. We laughed at them and we scorned them. And those of us who had any sense steered clear of working for them. Of course there were some devious tenant farmers, but I always found that on the whole they made better bosses. Perhaps this was because the laird and his factor were ruling their lives, so to speak, making sure that the farms were maintained and kept in good heart and repair along the lines of the terms of their lease. Perhaps having someone to order them about made sure they treated us better. I don't know. But it was a fact that they were better. But whether owners or tenants, there were far too many greedy and miserly figures among them, fellows who would have the last drop of sweat from you and in return see to it that you, the workman, got no more than the absolute minimum in wages, and for the likes of me, a single man and living-in, the bare necessities of comfort and food.

Still, right from the start, after my experience with the farmer who cheated the grieve, I was wary. I kept my ears open for word of the good farmers in the district who had some respect for the honest workman, those who, though they might work you hard, were always fair and never expected the impossible. And who, at the end of the term, would pay up without fuss. Of course I got to hear of all the bad ones, too, and when hiring day came (the last Friday in May and November) and I was there in the town along with all the other farm workers in the area seeking new jobs, I'd keep a good watch for any of them approaching. If I was asked by one of them if I wanted a job with him I'd make some excuse or other and off he'd go elsewhere — in search of some other hapless soul. Mind you, you soon learned to keep on the move so that you seldom came into contact with any of them and after a time when farmers got to hear about you and they knew you were a good worker there might be two or even three all seeking to hire you at the same time.

The hiring day was called "Muckle Friday" and in every market town the workers gathered who were looking for jobs — and the farmers seeking to engage them. Sometimes we all congregated in the square or in a street close-by where the markets were held. In Aberdeen it was always in the Castlegate. There were all sorts there — shepherds, horsemen, cattlemen, general labourers (orramen as they used to be called in these parts). Then all the farmers would come along. One might stop in front of you and ask if you were looking for a job. You'd say, "Aye, that's right." And from

40

then on you were in business. You told him what you could do — what previous experience you had. He told you how much he was prepared to offer you to do it. Then, as he talked, you thought about it, at the same time trying to weigh-up in your mind what sort of bloke he might be. You quickly learned to be a good judge of character, but even then mistakes could be made. Some farmers wore different faces on hiring days, a wee bit like Robert Louis Stevenson's Dr Jekyll and Mr Hyde. They had one face for "Muckle Friday" which was all smiles and heartiness. And a week later, once you were there on the farm working for them, you saw the other side of their nature, always glowering and moaning, greedy and grasping. Yes, you made mistakes, but they got fewer as you got older. I suppose you just got wiser, that's all. Anyhow, when both sides were satisfied and terms were agreed, you shook hands. That hand-clasp sealed the bargain. It was a promise on both sides. No man worth his salt — farmer or worker — would ever have gone back on that.

As I've said, you soon learned to watch out for the good farmers in the district and they often came after you when you got a name for yourself as a responsible worker. And, of course, once having got hold of you they would do all in their power to keep you on their farm. This meant that at the end of the term they would offer you an increase in wages and if you were happy with the work and the new money and could see no point in leaving to seek another job, which, after all, might not be so good, you'd just stay on. But it was always a one-sided business. So much depended on the whims and fancies of the farmer. You were beholden to him for too much of your life. It was worse for a married man because he would be living with his wife and children in one of the farm cottages. Naturally, with family responsibilities he didn't want to be moving around from place to place every summer and winter. And if anything happened that made the boss decide not to hire him again for the new term, there he was, not only having to seek a new job, but without a roof over his head until he found one. At the end of the term he would have to be out of the cottage he lived in in order to make room for the chap who was taking his place. Many the cart load of furniture and belongings, with wee kids sitting on top of them and the crying mother in front sitting beside her grim-faced husband, I've seen disappearing down the road from the farm.

A man could get pretty desperate having to put up with all these extra problems on top of having to work hard in all sorts of weather. He daren't argue with his boss, he could not afford to let his health go, for a sick man had no chance once some bad illness had set in. And above all, out of the money he was getting he had to try to save something to help him out when some disaster occurred or when he got too old to go on working. The odds were very much against him. It was a constant struggle.

Nowadays, though I still think the basic wage for agricultural workers could be higher, a man working on a farm has none of the worries we old ones had in the past. Oh yes, he'll have his problems. Who hasn't, living in such a world with prices rising every five minutes? But his job is secure. He would have to be a proper scoundrel — or a shirker — to find himself being given the sack and even then his boss would have to make out a good case, strong enough to stand up to enquiry by a tribunal, if the worker decided to fight. And another thing, on top of his minimum wage, he'll receive extra for being a specialist in a particular job — craftsman

42

they call it — if he's in charge of a herd of cows, looking after a pig unit, a tractor driver even. And what's more, when he works a minute over the laid-down number of hours he'll receive overtime pay. Now that's something we never had, nor did we even think about it.

The standard hours of work in my early days were ten hours a day, six days a week, Monday to Saturday, but at times, such as during the harvest, you just had to work on until bed-time, especially if the weather had been bad and the crops were late in being cut. And you got no pay for this extra work. No overtime. It had never been heard of. You just carried on, slogging away until the job was finished. The farmer was keen because he wanted it safely stacked in the yard, the workers because they were damned glad to get rid of it. If you'd had three weeks of "stook parade", when we had to gather in all the sheaves, and you were soaking wet up to the armpits many a day when it had been raining heavily, you were bloody glad to see the stooks off the field. That was compensation enough for all the extra hard graft.

It was all hands on deck at harvest time — the "hairst" as we called it. The farmer would have one eye on the weather and the other on the ripening grain, usually corn. All of a sudden he would announce, "We're starting on Monday, boys." So, the first job was to clear a road right around the edge of the field using a scythe. Then the binder could get in. In a way I was lucky. Binders were being used on practically every farm I worked on. But before this, at the time of the reaper, all the cut stalks had to be lifted by hand, bound into sheaves, then stooked so that it could dry off in the sun before being carted away to the farm stackyard. Of course now it's combine harvesters everywhere, but in my day the crops weren't so heavy, though at the end of a long day, with your back aching and your fingers full of thistles, you thought the crop heavy enough, I can tell you.

To give you an instance of how machines were getting a hold on farm work when I started, I remember a day in 1914 when I saw four different styles of harvesting being done — all within sight of each other. On a wee croft there was an old widow woman going at her little bit of corn, back bent cutting it with a sickle; next door an old chap with another croft was cutting his with a reaper. Then, on the other side of the road the local carpenter and joiner was working with a scythe on his croft, while next to him we were there working with the binder. Four different ways of doing the job, from the oldest method of all to the most modern. And that was 1914, just after the start of the Great War.

When all the corn was threshed and turned into grain and straw this was another time of great activity. The stackyard was filled with people, each man with a particular job to do, from those who forked the sheaves off the stacks and into the maws of the threshing mill to the youngsters, who with the dogs chased and killed the rats running for fresh shelter in other parts of the farm. The threshing machine was normally a traction engine with the mill attached to it. A number of farmers in the district would hire it and round it would go from farm to farm. What a devil of a noise it made, belching steam and smoke and rattling all over, the whole engine shaking and snarling as behind it the threshing mill clattered on amid a cloud of dust and chaff from the new-milled grain. Your clothes would be white with the dust. It got in your eyes and up your nose and in your ears. It would be there for days afterwards — long after the mill had gone.

I don't know what was the hardest job to be done on threshing days. There would be two men forking the sheaves up onto the mill, two men cutting the string binding the sheaves, one man feeding them into the mill, two men down there among the grain seeing to the sacks, dragging away the full ones and replacing them (you'd to be a real nifty hand at this job otherwise the grain would have been all over the place). Then three or four men would be alongside forking up the straw to another couple whose job was to build it into mounds. And all round about there would be others seeing to the traction engine, carrying coal, feeding the fire, filling the boiler with water. Oh yes, there was plenty of work to be done by those willing to do it at threshing time. You needed every pair of hands available if a successful threshing was to be managed in the time the engine and mill was with you. Because of this the farmers used to get together and combine their work forces and we all travelled around in a great gang going from farm to farm at this time of year.

There were other times when there was plenty of extra work to be done; when the sowing and planting was on in the spring, thinning turnip plants with a long-handled hoe, lifting potatoes, this sort of thing. Fighting the weather and trying to beat it — that was all part of the job. But damn the extra penny for it did I ever see.

However, when I was a young man we started to get a half-day off (a Saturday afternoon) every week from about the end of June up to the start of the harvest. But when the harvest got underway it was back to your full six days work again. That was the start of the half-days on the farms — just for two or three months of the year. Then, in the winter six-month term you might get two or three weekends off during this time — from a Friday night to the Sunday night. But this often depended on the generosity of the farmer. Mind you, it had its drawbacks for a single man like I was then. I was being fed by the farmer's wife and slept there of course. But when they gave you a weekend off you had to clear out — get away from the farm. You didn't get your food. They didn't give you a holiday and give you your meat too, you know. Not even the best of farmers was generous enough to stretch things that far. If you weren't working there was no food for you, so off you had to go. And the strange thing is, none of us used to ever give this a second thought. We never used to say to ourselves or each other — "Whichever way we turn we're not getting a fair deal." It never crossed my mind that we should be working an eight-hour day instead of ten; that we should be getting paid more for working extra time for the farmer; that there should be fixed holidays and more generous time off. I just accepted the position as it was. We all accepted it. Least, most of us did. Oh yes, a few grumbled. Some of us used to think they were trouble-makers. Now, I'm not so sure. Perhaps they were right and we were wrong. Who knows?

And you know, when we first got our half-day off every week between June and the start of the harvest I found it more of a nuisance than anything else. It was all right if you had any money to spend, but if you had nothing in your pocket it wasn't much of a holiday. And most times, the young chaps like me never had any money. Least, I never had. You got paid at the end of the six-month term — not weekly or monthly as it is now. Just twice a year. On the 28th day of May and the 28th day of November the farmer would come out to whatever part of the farm you happened to be working on and he'd hand you your money. If you were staying on for another six months you'd have already made a fresh bargain with him. If you were leaving — you just left there and then, after receiving your wages.

The strange thing is that when I look back like this it all seems to have been a time of hardship and worry, of grimness. Oh yes, it had its bad moments, but there was a lot of fun to be had, too. On a good farm it was like being a member of a big, happy family where everybody knew each other really well and no one would ever think of shirking because they'd be letting down their mates. There was a lot of respect, too, not only for the boss, if he was a decent man, but between the boss and his workers and among the workers themselves. When someone was in a senior position to you it was usually because he was more skilled than you were. And you respected him for this. I think much of that attitude is gone today from farm life.

Today's worker may have better conditions, money, holidays, pension schemes and such like, but that spirit of comradeship such as I knew it is missing from his life. I suppose it's just a sign of the times. In a world of machines and so-called efficiency and productivity such as you hear every farmer preaching about nowadays, there's little time for a laugh — precious little to laugh about. And when a man is able to get overtime pay there's never the same urge, as we all felt, to get on and finish the job not because we'd be any richer, but simply because we thought it should be done. I'm glad men are paid now for every minute of their efforts. In this way no one can be taken advantage of, in the way that many of us were. But we felt some pride in doing a job well and, sad to say, pride in workmanship is not very obvious on the vast majority of farms nowadays. In a way the boot's on the other foot now. It's not the farmer who can take advantage of his workers (he's got little scope for that with all the rules and regulations) but the men who can take advantage of the farmer. It happens all over — in other walks of life. But I'm sad to see it happening on farms.

I mentioned taking a pride in the job. One example of this was the horseman. You had to rise every morning at 4.45 and give your horses a feed and sort them, ready for the day's work. You'd then go into the farmhouse at 5.30 to have your breakfast and be out again, ready to start work at 6.00. You might be ploughing, or harrowing, or sowing, depending on the time of year, and after five hours you'd stop at 11.00. Then for the next two hours you had to groom your horses and have your dinner. In the middle of this time you'd go into the house to eat, then back out to the stables to continue with the grooming and feeding until 1.00. Away you went again to work in the fields until 6.00 in the evening. It was then back to the stables to sort out your horses, brush them down, feed them and into the house to have your supper at 6.30p.m. Then at 9p.m. you always went to your horses to feed them again before they got settled for the night.

On the usual farm there would be three pairs of horses — one pair to each man. And in addition to all the work in just looking after the animals, apart from the farm work, there would be all the tackle, the harness, bridle, reins and what like, to keep in good repair and to clean and polish. Horsemen were dedicated people. A breed apart from other men. No amount of money could ever have been enough to pay a man to work all those hours of the day and night. Least, nowadays you'd be hard put to find a man willing to do it even if he was being well paid to do such a job. But you see, the true horseman was never thinking about money. He liked working with horses. That's why he did the job. And he took pride in seeing to it that they were well fed, groomed and turned out. To see a pair of Clydesdales with the brasses gleaming and the plough behind them, the furrow straight as a die, made you feel proud just to look at them. The best horsemen always had the best looking beasts. Their ploughing was always neater than anyone else's. Even when it came to building a stack you'd find that their stacks were better finished than their neighbours'. You see, this pride in doing a job really well, pride in making sure that their work was a cut above the others, was inside the real horseman right from the moment they got their chance, sometimes as a youngster, to handle their first pair of horses. They were magnificent beasts, the

old farm horses. They looked proud themselves. This pride infected the men charged with caring for them and working them in all weather, at every time of the year. And, somehow, in a curious way this pride they had infected us all. If you didn't feel it in your heart then you were not suitable for working on a farm.

That's how I felt, but I'm damn sure there would be few who could say such a thing today. Not now. Not now that the spirit has gone from farm life. Blown away like the chaff at threshing time. Vanished — just like the horses.

CHAPTER
FOUR

In the winter months the river flows through Strathalder on its journey to the sea as if, somehow, time was against it. It is a rushing, cascading torrent of white foam and brown water heavily stained by the peaty soil of the moor. On the mountain slopes and in the corries and gullies pockmarking the moorland the snow melts and seeps into the tiny burns. They lead to the river where it meanders through the moor, the source of it being a mere crack in the earth between two great rocks, the water trickling to freedom from far within the depths of the mountain.

For most of the year up here on the moor the river is gentle, the water running quietly over fine shingle and sand, so clear and pure that on a summer's day the slightest shadow will send the brown trout and fry darting for shelter beneath the overhanging banks. The salmon make long, tortuous journeys upstream from the sea to spawn in the crystal-clear water; generation upon generation of fish, starting life as fry, becoming parr, then grilse, to emerge as fully-grown salmon, returning by the power of an inherent instinct which draws them back to the place of their birth. Their spawning completed, the fish move away downstream, the females thin and emaciated, exhausted by the effort of egg laying, the male fish no longer gleaming like silver bars, their scales now tinged with red, like a coating of rust. Back to the sea they go once more, through the torrents and over the waterfalls, gliding unseen in the depths of the quieter pools far down in the valley, at times their return journey more arduous because of their weakness than when they first homed towards the upland river several months previously.

Unlike so many features of Strathalder estate the river has always been there; a part of the landscape, unchanging, while all around it forests have grown and been felled and trees have been planted again and houses and roads, trackways and paths have been placed upon the face of the earth by the manipulating hand of man. Over the centuries the gorges may have become deeper, here and there a slight change of course where the constant action of the rushing water has eroded the soil at a bend; but for the most part had you been around to walk the length of its course in, say, the eighteenth century, in 1745 at the time of Bonnie Prince Charlie and his fight for the Crown, then you would have walked the same route as that taken by someone today. It is said that some minor skirmishes took place along the banks of the river between clansmen and English soldiers. There is a legend that speaks of a desperate leap by a fleeing Jacobite officer who, in order to escape his pursuers, jumped to freedom across the yawning mouth of a deep and sinister gorge. No documents record this happening. It is merely spoken about, a moment from the past. It could well be true. There are few Scottish rivers without such stories attached to them, tales of bravado and daring where the turbulence of the river and its qualities of power and abounding strength claw at the imagination and make one want to believe.

The river flows through the estate in a variety of moods. From the moorland it plunges into a narrow wooded glen, birch and alder, pine and rowan, hugging the steep boulder-strewn banks, going down and down, a waterborne staircase leading to the floor of the valley below. Here, the pools are narrow and deep, connected by rushing channels, miniature waterfalls among the rocks. The salmon run swiftly where the water boils in madness, but rest from their efforts in the ink-black depths of the silent pools. This is the part of the river frequented by only the most experienced, or perhaps at times the most foolhardy, angler. No path exists. The only means of getting from pool to pool is by scrambling over the rocks, clutching here and there for support at a variety of handholds, boulders, the trunks of trees, at times mere tussocks of heather with roots embedded firmly in the arid soil. To follow the river in the wildest part of the glen, amid the haunt of red deer and wildcat, is a journey for the most sure-footed, the person with balance and sense; someone with the awareness that here the terrain is the master with scant regard for the foolish and the unwary.

For the fisherman, with boots and rod and all the tackle necessary to the angler, negotiating this stretch of the river and actually fishing it is a feat of endurance. But the rewards can be great; not only in terms of the catch, but through the joy gained from overcoming the difficult countryside and fishing where every single movement of line and cast across the water is a test of skill. The salmon lie in the deepest pools, lurking in the quiet water at the base of the rocks, brown trout leap at the flies and insects hatching from the foliage edging the banks. In order to catch a fish the angler must keep his line away from the trees crowding his back, see that the artificial fly does not snag on a hundred and one obstacles. But when he succeeds and the thump has come, the boil in the water as the fish strikes, the line tightens and the reel screams, he knows the true meaning of what it is to be a hunter. In water such as this the hooked fish has every advantage, able to use the length and breadth of the pool to escape, while his adversary must tread with care as he follows close to the water's edge.

In the more shallow pools the sons of shepherds and farmers on the moor, when such a place was inhabited, would come and lie on their stomachs alongside the river and "tickle" the trout up and out and on to the bank. Many lads perfected this means of catching a breakfast, using stealth and skill and great patience; once spotted basking on the bed of shingle a hand would enter the water downstream of the fish, then slide slowly under the belly, caressing, stroking. Surprisingly, few trout escaped the grasping fingers of a skilled exponent. Before they could sense the danger and dart away the hand had closed around them and they were out of the water and on the bank beside a grinning youngster. It was a skill that was almost an art. It is now forgotten.

The river leaves the moorland behind and flows through woods and among fields, close to the main road and the now disused railway line. It passes under several bridges, some modern, a couple erected in late Victorian times and one built by General George Wade to allow the free passage of the military forces policing the Highlands of Scotland after the Jacobite Rebellion of 1715. Being close to a road, this stretch of river is particularly vulnerable to poachers; not the old-style "one for the pot" merchants, but gangs from distant towns and cities who arrive in vans at dead of night and empty their cans of poisonous powdered gas into the pools. The critical time comes in the early part of the year when the nights are long and the salmon, fresh from the sea, are cramming the pools as they move upstream following their relentless course. It only takes an hour or so to contaminate a pool with gas (which sends every fish in it floating to the surface) haul them to the bank and into sacks, then away, leaving a sweet, sickly stench in the air and the bodies of those fish unwanted by the poachers littering the surface of the water. Patrols are made by river authority bailiffs and the gamekeeper and his fishing gillies, but it is a long river and impossible to guard absolutely effectively.

A few poachers are caught — and fined — but usually for being in illegal possession of salmon. Very few gangs are ever detected engaged in the act of removing fish from the water. Their own security is usually too good for that to happen. Greed is the driving force behind such poaching nowadays, not the thrill of pitting wits against those of the gamekeeper for the pure pleasure and excitement to be gained from lifting a fish from the laird's river; or, as was sometimes the case, a need to supplement the meagre diet of a family too large to exist on what was provided in the normal course of events. The old-style poacher was certainly considered a nuisance. At times he was even quite ruthlessly dissuaded from following his activities, depending on the mood and level of toleration of the laird or his head gamekeeper. One habitual poacher had his fishing rod smashed in two by a blast from a twelve bore shotgun, the gamekeeper lurking behind him in the bushes as he fished in the middle of the night on one of the best pools on the estate. The poacher never returned. But although a state of war existed between both sides there remained an element of goodwill, even toleration up to a point. Now, the poachers who hunt in packs are hated, not just because of the despicable methods they use, but because it is no longer possible, due to a shortage of staff, to combat their activities with absolute success. The modern gamekeeper or fishing gillie will possibly laugh when he discovers an illicit angler using rod and line. Quite likely he will merely admonish him and send him on his way, whereas in the past an appearance before a magistrate or even in a higher court before a sheriff would have been guaranteed. But give him a hint that a gang is in the area and he will shun all rest until he is able to put a stop to their work. It is often a useless and thankless task. As with most things in the modern world, money rules the day when it comes to salmon poaching. Quite often the gangs have considerable wealth behind them and the money they can earn from the sale of the fish is vast. Unfortunately, for Strathalder, as with many estates, money is not available to curb successfully the activities of the mobile poachers at a time when their influence is steadily growing.

The river runs in a wide curve less than one hundred yards from the mansion house. There is a flat expanse of lawn stretching from a rockery to the fringes of the river bank, the rippling stream kept at bay by means of a sloping wall of stones and rubble set in a concrete fastness. It is a reminder of what happened a little more than two decades ago when a flood tore away the bank and sent the river across the lawn. It was the worst flood since late Victorian times — 1891 or thereabouts. For seventy-two hours the rain fell unceasingly. At first the river rose slowly, then as the storm increased the height gathered momentum until the roar of the swollen water could be heard like the distant, persistent rumble of thunder. The soil ran freely from the high banks and was washed away by the rain, trees became dislodged and toppled into the river. Caught in the flood the trees were carried downstream, bumping and crashing their way through the gorges; wooden bridges, linking one side of the estate to the other, were swept away and splintered and fragmented within minutes. Within thirty-six hours the estate was facing chaos and havoc from the river, now unleashing a power which could not be halted. It was truly a force of destruction.

Here and there tree trunks became jammed in narrow passages between the banks, forcing the river to change course, and in this fashion it swept across the lawn in front of the mansion house, throwing boulders into the air, gouging holes, destroying an ornamental pond, before cutting a channel among the trees and running back into its original course.

Estate workers were powerless to act. The forces of Nature had proved, once again, to be impervious to the will of Man; and, as if to emphasize the point, caused such devastation to paths and river banks, bridges and woodland that some of the damage could never be put right, so great was the cost. When, eventually, the rain ceased and the flooded river returned slowly to normality the lawn in front of the mansion house resembled an area pock-marked by bomb craters, the holes filled with salmon and trout, some still alive in the muddy water. But many were dead, adding to the several hundreds found lying on banks and in ditches in the woods flanking the river.

The river has remained within its bounds ever since. Fortunately, such a flood is an extremely rare occurrence. Occasionally, in the months of winter, the river shows signs of its former fury, but although it rises and roars there is no more flooding. In summer it presents an image of tranquil charm as it winds its way through the wooded grounds of the estate. Hazel and alder grow on the banks, pines and beech, fir and birch throw canopies of shade over some of its pools. In the early morning it may be possible to catch a glimpse of an otter swimming at ease in a favourite pool. Dippers and wagtails bob and display, catch insects from rocks in mid-stream. At dusk the long, hungry shape of a heron glides in to feed in silence, a hunched shape on long legs poised to strike with vicious bill when any trout or salmon parr swims within range.

Houses have crumbled and people have come and gone, the pattern of estate life has been changed gradually by the passage of time. But of all things within the bounds of Strathalder the river remains constant, providing a feature of beauty and permanancy and, now that salmon fishing has become more than just a sport for the rich, a valuable source of income. What was once the object of pleasure is now a much prized commercial asset.

CHAPTER
FIVE

On a river prized for its salmon, whether fished by the laird for his own pleasure and that of his personal guests, or rented to a variety of fishermen throughout the year, the key factor to success is the employment of a first-class, highly experienced gillie. Contrary to popular and romantic thought, he is not merely the man who carries the fishing tackle and who lands the hooked fish or is obsessed day and night by the thought of poachers raiding the riches in his river. All these things he certainly does, but in order to accomplish them he must bear the stamp of the dedicated craftsman.

His fishing year usually begins in February, in winter's coldest month, when the salmon season opens and continues until the end of September. However, although the angling may be over the gillie's work goes on. There are roads and paths alongside the river to be repaired, trees to be trimmed or felled where their branches seriously interfere with anglers' lines, banks to be renovated and built up where flood water has weakened or torn them away, perhaps even modifications to be made to pools which might make them more amenable to fish in search of a resting place as they move upstream. This can, at times, be a relatively simple job; the action of rolling a large boulder into a pool has been known to turn a useless part of the river into a highly attractive section for resting salmon. More usually, when substantial work requires to be done it is undertaken by a bulldozer or mechanical digger capable of shifting tons of boulders and rocks, manoeuvring them into their new position in several feet of running water. To plan and supervise such work requires a keen eye and a strict attention to detail if the shape of the pool and the flow of the water is not to be ruined. The experienced gillie is well aware of the dangers and before embarking on this will spend a considerable time judging what has to be done and how best to do it.

Unlike the gamekeeper and the shepherd who, more often than not, spend their working days in solitude, accompanied only by a dog, the gillie is usually a more extrovert person. He is expected to enjoy the company of others. If he does not, then he must make every effort to appear that he does. He must present the image of being a sociable person. His prime function on the estate river during the fishing season is to give service and satisfaction to the innumerable guests; to ensure that they are all given the maximum opportunity to hook and land the salmon they have come to the river to catch. At times it is an impossible and infuriating task. Fishing guests come in all shapes, sizes and temperaments. The gillie is expected to treat all alike, but, in effect, has his own subtle way of handling those who prove incapable of following the rules. To the

difficult guest he may not be quite so free with the considerable amount of information he carries in his head about the river and the movements of the fish. It is this acquired knowledge that is the hallmark of the gillie's success; the secret of his expertise.

Andrew Fraser, once a gamekeeper, now the head fishing gillie, has no doubts on this aspect of his job. He has studied his river, the salmon and the men and women who come to catch them. He finds them all fascinating, but admits that the knowledge he requires in order to do his job successfully is something he has absorbed, detail by detail, as the years have passed.

The knowledge a good gillie carries in his head about his river is enormous. Quite frankly there is so much I doubt if I could explain even the half of it. It takes years and years of patient study. It just goes on and on. And it will never end. I'm certain of this. I am still learning something fresh and new about methods of fishing and about the river and the fish themselves. A gillie must be prepared to adapt and as far as possible keep an open mind. This is especially so when it comes to dealing with the differing abilities of the many guests I have fishing here with me every year. I think the main thing is that a gillie must be a bit of a diplomat in order to do his job properly. All the same, he must never be afraid to speak his mind if a guest steps out of line and is not obeying the rules of fishing as they apply to the river here on this estate. He carries a trump card all the time: this knowledge of the river he possesses. It can mean everything to the guest if he is going to start catching fish without wasting too much time. I always think that the sooner a guest realizes and appreciates this fact then the better for all concerned.

A gillie has to know and understand many things. He has to know when the fish are running, where and when they will rest at different times of the year and how they are likely to be affected by changing conditions in the level of the river and the temperature of the water. The temperature must be taken every day. There's a great deal of information to be gained from it and depending on what it is the gillie will have some idea of what size of fly to recommend or, if in the early part of the year, whether or not it is only worthwhile because of the cold to use a spinning rod. A gillie who is really absorbed in his job will take every opportunity to watch the river, the fish and the direction of the wind. He should also be fully familiar with every pool and stream on his beat on the river — their depth, the lie of the fish and the state of the river which suits the fish best of all. In addition to this he must know the effect of the sun upon the pools (there's nothing worse for frightening salmon away), the direction of the wind that catches certain of them and the best side from which the pool can be fished at any particular time of the day.

Every day before going to the river — his first job in the morning — he has to check tackle, rods, reels, lines, flies, casts and baits which have been provided for the fishing. He will then be able to advise the guests about the best rod to use, the most suitable line — either one that floats on the surface or one that sinks well beneath it — the particular size of fly for the height of the water that day. He has one hundred and one things to remember to do and years ago there was a rhyme which young gillies used to be advised to learn by heart to help them become familiar with this part of their day's work. It goes like this:

Rods, reels and hooks,
Nets, bait and baskets,
Gaff, baton, books,
Coats, lunch and flaskets.

The gaff — a long pole with a sharp metal hook — is what is used to lift the fish out of the water and on to the bank after the fisherman has tired the salmon sufficiently in order to bring it close in to the water's edge. It's often used in preference to a net. The baton referred to is a short, truncheon-like club for striking the head of the salmon in order to kill it. Books aren't what most folks will think — for reading when the fishing is poor — but fly-books containing dozens of different salmon flies in all sizes and colours. Flaskets is just another word for whisky flasks — spirit flasks really, but as whisky is the most popular drink among anglers in these parts then this is what they would contain. Mind you, today he doesn't have to worry about the flaskets. That's a throw-back to the old days when the gillie was looking after the laird and his personal guests staying in the Big House. Today's guests are different. They are paying for their sport. They bring their own whisky and dispense it according to their own nature — generous or otherwise.

When the various guests have been allocated their pools to fish and the serious business of actually fishing is underway, the gillie remains on hand to offer advice and assist where necessary should any angler get into difficulty or require help in landing a fish. In the old days, when staffs were large on estates, practically every guest fishing the river would have had his own personal gillie for the day or the week or however long he was staying. Nowadays, one gillie might be required to look after everyone. Most days when the fishing is at its best, in the peak of the season, there will be up to six rods covering the best pools on the river. So, he tries to give everyone a part of his day, going back and fore between them all. Some demand more attention than others because they're not very experienced, while many will be perfectly happy to cope and to solve their own problems as they arise. The real fisherman — the true sportsman — and the man or woman whom the gillie sees as the ideal guest, is the person who listens to his advice and who is content to get on with fishing no matter the condition of weather or river; in fact, the person who has a deep regard and feeling for the river and the opportunity for catching salmon every bit as much as the gillie himself. Fortunately, there are still plenty of people around who take their fishing seriously and feel this way. It is a joy to work with them.

A gillie comes to love his stretch of the river, his beat as he calls it. It is his own special territory, his very own piece of the estate and unlike the gamekeeper, who probably has the entire estate to cover, with many different things to do, the gillie can devote his entire attention to making sure that his domain is as efficient and as neat as possible. The difference between a good, experienced gillie and the man who really couldn't care less about his job, or who has never bothered to master it thoroughly, is enormous. To a guest it can be the difference between an enjoyable fishing holiday, whether or not many salmon have been caught, and one spent in a state of constant frustration. And now that it's important for the

66

estate to secure a high income from letting the fishing throughout the season, the gillie must be a good one if things are to prosper and develop. If he's reliable and good at his job then the guest will depart a satisfied man — and he'll be back, either later in the season or the following year; perhaps for years to come. In many ways a good gillie is an ambassador. At least that's how I see it. Very often, the fishing guests never see or meet the laird. Their bookings are handled by the factor in the estate office and the first, and perhaps the only person they ever see on the estate, is the gillie. On some estates the guests are in contact with the gillie's wife as well, where there's a lodge and she does the cooking for them.

Many guests become personal friends of both the gillie and his wife in this way so that a happy atmosphere prevails on both sides. I've heard it said that a good gillie is worth his weight in gold to a laird. I think I'd like to include the wife in this statement as well. Whether or not she has to play any direct part in caring for the guests she is always on call, just like her husband. Fishermen have little regard for the hours of the day if the salmon are running and there are fish to be caught. She may have her husband's dinner prepared, the meal nicely cooked, ready to be eaten and he doesn't turn up for it. He may be out somewhere and she has to deal on her own with visits from fishermen who have booked for later in the season and just come along to have a look at the stretch of river they have rented. I doubt if any gillies' wives have ever fished in their lives, but you'll find that the best of them, just like their husbands, will know every bit of the river and what goes on and what should be done in this pool or that. Like their husbands they, too, are dedicated. They live for their river. It is their life.

On Strathalder the fishing is let by the week although towards the tail-end of the season when there's fewer salmon around there are day lettings done as well for a few weeks. But the spring and early summer are the really busy months. And in February, when the season opens, the river is usually running very high, almost in a state of flood. That's the time for big log fires in the fishing huts on the banks of the river where the guests can go during the day to get out of the wind and the rain, or, more often than not, the snow. There are days when the water is full of grue — floating ice that has come down from the mountains — but although it may be cold and your teeth are chattering you know that out there in the river, somewhere out of sight among the rocks, are the really big fish. What fighters they are when they're hooked. Some may only have been in the river a matter of hours. Once caught, you can always tell a really fresh salmon because it will have sea lice on its scales. They can only live for a short time in fresh water — forty-eight hours at the most — and after this will have dropped off to leave the salmon completely clean. The majority of the really big salmon are caught at this time of year, those in the 30lb range — great, strong fish, full of energy and life after their rich feeding in the sea. They take quite a bit of handling when you've got one on the end of your line. But they're a real challenge.

Mind you, the sea trout which run up the river at the end of May and in June are also very exciting to get a hold of. They're extremely agile fish, darting about all over the pool, leaping right out of the water, as they try to shake the hook out of their mouth. In many ways it can sometimes be more

of a thrill to catch and play a lively sea trout than to get hold
of a salmon. The salmon can be a very dour fish at times and
with a heavy rod and strong cast with a hefty breaking-strain,
the odds on losing him, if you follow all the rules, are
negligible. But with a sea trout, hooked on a light line and
cast on a small trout rod, then it's another matter entirely. His
actions have to be countered every inch of the way. He'll
practically dance along the surface of the water, try every trick
in the book, to escape from you. He's the best fighter of all
the fish and as a result he very often gets away. Full of action
he is. And quite often, the best time for catching sea trout
being around dusk, you're there on the bank of the river in the
pitch dark and instead of seeing what is going on you can
only judge by feel and the sound of the reel screaming and
the splashing somewhere in the pool in front of you. To my
mind that is the most magnificent sport of all; a fine June
evening with the sound of rising sea trout "boiling" the
surface of the pool as they leap at the last hatch of flies of the
day; and then, to have one on the end of your line for five, or
perhaps ten minutes of the most glorious battle you'll ever
know as a fisherman. It's a thrill every time. There's no doubt
about it.

The changes that have come about in the salmon fishing
on this estate have been tremendous over the years. The
gillie's job is probably the one where the most jealousy can be
generated on the entire estate. The competition is fierce.
Gillies vie with each other about the numbers of the various
catches, the sizes of salmon, this sort of thing. And if a gillie
or the paying guest, as it is nowadays, who is with him is
getting more fish than the others all sorts of suspicions are

put forward that foul means are being used to achieve such success. It just reeks with suspicion.

Now, in the old days, the 1920s and 1930s and even later, people used to come here and take the water and pay a rent of between £15 and £20 a week. In those days a gillie's wage would have been in the region of £3 a week. The salmon value in the late twenties and early thirties was only about 2s.6d. a pound. As a result fish were given away to people living on the estate or sent off to relatives and friends. The staff in the Big House were often feeding on salmon themselves, there was so much fish about. There were even estates where, when house staff were engaged, there would be a clause inserted in their agreement to say that they wouldn't receive meals of salmon or venison more than twice a week. So, with so much fish to spare there was no cause for jealousy among those responsible for catching them.

It was a recognized and accepted fact that if you caught, say, four fish today then luck might have it that you might only get one tomorrow. On the other hand, the other gillie with his guest further up the river, say, might do the reverse. Today, everything is spoiled because of the massive rents — sums like £80 to £200 a week, sometimes more — for one rod. The market at the opening of the season in February is a highly competitive one with a value of around £4 per pound for salmon. Even later on in the season, in late spring, May, early June, a salmon will fetch £2 per pound. This means that most people who rent fishing nowadays do it with the sole purpose of either covering their expenses or, if they're lucky, making a profit out of it.

At times the gillie is as much involved in all this as anyone else because of the general mercenary attitude pervading the

70

sport. In the pre-war days, yes, and for many years after the war, our guests were all people of some standing in life. They were true aristocrats. They were all people who had been brought up as gentlemen and sportsmen. They knew how to handle a gun and a fishing rod. But today, you've got the new rich showing themselves all over the place. They're taking over. They are now the ones renting most of the fishing. The old types — the ones who had all the money in the past — they can't afford it now. It's the new get-rich-quick people with all the money to splash around who dictate the terms and some of those whom you see salmon fishing today, well, in the past, the average water bailiff would have been checking up on a lot of them. They often look and behave more like poachers than fishing tenants. As a result far too much greed has crept into what was once one of the finest field sports.

It sometimes happens that, if a gillie is with one of this type who is not catching many fish for some reason or other, then the poor gillie gets all the blame for what the tenant describes as his poor sport. The reason is quite simple, really. This type of tenant rarely understands the complex behaviour of salmon or the changes that can come over a river in the space of a single night — rise and fall of the water, changes in temperature. You can get an excellent gillie who knows every trick of the trade, but in the long run it's the salmon who is the real master. Salmon have a great habit of being in the wrong place at the wrong time. And there's not a thing the gillie can do about it, no matter how good he is at his job. At the very same time the neighbouring gillie on the next beat might be totally inexperienced and just have the good fortune to be with his guest at a particular pool where the salmon are resting in good numbers. He just happens to be at the right spot at the right time, So he has success and gets plenty of credit.

One of the major changes has come about as a result of the difference in the type of person who now becomes a fishing gillie compared with in the past. The old type of gillie has

more or less died out altogether; the man who lived for his job and loved every minute of it. The man who was born into it. In the past the sons of gillies always fished themselves during the quiet time of the year and became really expert. They quickly began to learn every wrinkle there was to know about the art of salmon fishing and in the usual way, as with most estate jobs, it was tradition that they would follow their father and become fishing gillies themselves. This meant there was always a good, solid body of men, quite experienced at the start of their working lives, making sure that high standards were maintained on the river. But now, just like gamekeeping, anybody seems to get gillies' jobs. I have known four or five young chaps who were taken on and within a few days there they were, a couple of them on the best beats on the river, fully-fledged fishing gillies supposed to be advising their guests. Not a one among them had ever held a fishing rod in his hand before getting the job. None of them could even tie on a fly with a proper knot or make up a fresh cast to be attached to the line.

So, as you can see, the standard has dropped completely. I'm afraid that it's now at rock bottom. This is a state of affairs I hoped I'd never see in my own working life and as a result it makes me a sad man just to see it happen. Even to think about it.

CHAPTER
SIX

The long, winding driveway that twists and turns as it follows the course of the river from the main road in the strath to the front door of the mansion house once echoed to the pounding hooves of the laird's coach. The coachman and attendant footmen wore scarlet livery and looked proud as they swept between the massive gates, beneath the arch, on either side of the squat, granite lodge. There were stables for the horses in a wood close to the mansion house and the coachman and his wife lived alongside, while the grooms had their quarters above the buildings housing the laird's collection of carriages. It was a time of opulence and dignified magnificence.

When the era of the motor car dawned, the laird, being at that time by far the wealthiest individual in the district, was the first to bring the noise of a clattering engine and the smell of petrol fumes to this remote corner of Scotland. He amazed the locals, but then the laird, by virtue of his wealth, was a constant source of wonder to those who not only worked on his land but lived within the shadow of his influence. At first the novelty was such that the laird and the male members of his family drove themselves from place to place, but gradually as the role of coachman and groom faded into the dust of the past, ousted by this mechanical invention, the need grew for the services of someone whose enthusiasm for this new mode of transport matched that of his employer. At first it was this employee's skill in repairing defects and dealing with break-downs that was valued the most, but as the car became a common-place feature of life among the rich and the middle-classes, this new employee on the estate found himself adopting the position formerly held by the coachman; that of driving the laird, his family and guests wherever they cared to go. The chauffeur had been born.

As with most features of estate life, the period between the First and Second World Wars saw the pinnacle of achievement for the chauffeur. An extremely wealthy laird would almost certainly have retained two chauffeurs at that time — most likely one on the estate itself and one in the south attached to his city residence. Carrying out mechanical repairs, apart from minor problems, was no longer a part of the estate chauffeur's job. He was solely concerned with the task of driving and cleaning and polishing the fleet of vehicles at the laird's disposal — almost certainly one Bentley or a Rolls (sometimes both) and two other expensively upholstered and equally reliable saloons, the latest of the day.

After the Second World War the changed pattern of life for everyone was gradually reflected in the status of the chauffeur. The laird and his wife became accustomed to driving themselves, the chauffeur being used only when occasion demanded it, such as when a long journey was to be undertaken or attendance at a society function required some display of adherence to custom. As the years passed, the chauffeur's role diminished in estate service, as did the luxurious quality of the cars. Chauffeurs were expected once again to become familiar with the mechanical workings of their vehicles, to carry out servicing and light repairs. Today, the laird still leaves the estate on occasions with his chauffeur at the wheel of the car, but such instances are rare compared with the past.

John Jameson became a chauffeur because he enjoyed driving, but throughout his service on the estate spent more time behind the wheel of a heavy lorry ferrying cattle and sheep to market than in the driving seat of the laird's car.

I was born into estate life. As a child I was raised on an estate where my father was a gamekeeper. However, despite this close attachment to estate life, when I was about fourteen or so I decided I had no wish to work on one. It went against the grain to see my father working from six o'clock in the morning to six o'clock at night, right through, even longer — until it was dark — at the time of the pheasant rearing or grouse shooting, never having a spare minute to himself. I could see no future in this sort of existence. This was shortly before the Second World War — in the late thirties, 1936–37.

My father sort of expected I would follow in his footsteps and do estate work, but at the same time he was fully aware I had leanings towards doing something else. I was a bit indecisive. It took me ages to make up my mind about what I really wanted to do. I had lots of discussions with my father about my reasons for not wanting to do estate work. He was quite disappointed in me, I think. He thought it was a good life. He had never known anything else. I just thought he was wrong. I couldn't see anything in it at all for me. So eventually I said I was going to join the army. His reply was, "It's a tough life. You don't know what you're letting yourself in for." Anyway, that's what I did for twenty-two years before once again I found myself back on an estate.

When I was a child we lived in a very remote part of the estate, away out on the moors so, of course, apart from my schooldays I saw very little of the rest of the world. I suppose this made me even more eager to see something of life beyond the estate. When I joined the army I wanted to be a driver, lorries or cars; just driving. And in a way this was as a result of seeing my first really splendid car. I came home from school one afternoon and there was a great big car, a big Ford, sitting outside. It belonged to the laird. I had never been inside a car up to then — my father didn't have one, either for himself or for his work. I stood and gaped at it and I can distinctly remember thinking how I would like to be able to drive it. I was struck dumb for a time. Just by the sight of it. This great big car, very long, with beautiful chrome on it around the headlamps and on the bumpers. The coachwork was gleaming, the paint shining so vividly I could see my reflection in one of the doors. And sitting behind the steering wheel was the chauffeur waiting for the laird, who was in the house seeing my father and mother about something. He spoke to me and it was like being addressed by a foreigner. I couldn't understand a word he was saying. It was the first time I'd spoken to an Englishman — he was from London, I think. The boot was on the other foot, mind you. With my broad Scottish accent he couldn't understand me. All the same, he could see I was interested in this magnificent car so he let me have a good look at it, even at the engine and just for a minute the chance to sit in the driving seat and put my hands on the steering wheel. I was only a little boy then, but that car and the sight of the chauffeur in his immaculate uniform, something about both things, stuck in my mind for years. So, when I joined the army and learned to drive, the urge to want to do so must have stemmed from that happy day away back in my childhood.

As a youngster I came in contact with the laird's family — a boy and a girl — quite a bit, when the school holidays were on and they were back from the south where they went to boarding schools. I had been lectured time and again by my father and mother that if I ever met them I was to call them "Miss" and "Master". They were the boss's family and had to be given respect. Also that there were certain places in the estate grounds close to the Big House where I was not to go. Those parts of the garden were private and not for the likes of me. I think all the estate workers' children were told such things at some time or other, but like all kids we only took notice of what we wanted to heed. The laird's children were told the same thing, I suppose, but anyway we did meet up sooner or later despite how much all the adults on both sides wanted to keep us apart.

They were very good, the pair of them. Good fun to be with. In fact the young lad was a very pleasant, friendly boy about the same age as myself. He was an adventurous type, always keen on exploring the estate, climbing trees, looking for birds' nests, doing all the things country kids want to do.

He seemed keen to know all about me and how I spent my time. So, too, did his sister. They were extremely friendly. No doubt this good nature they both had came from their father. He was very good himself and took a great interest in all his workers. But the mother, the laird's wife, I can only shake my head when I think of her. She was a proper snob. She hated to think that her children would be having anything to do with the workers' children. This made us secretive, of course, so that the adults on both sides of the fence, as it were, would not find out.

I remember that once a few of us were playing hide and seek in the shrubbery when she discovered us. She was out for a walk and was strolling through the wood with one of the dogs. One minute we were all playing quite happily, the next there she was right in the middle of our game, with a glowering face and a sharp tongue, ordering her children to come back to the Big House with her. I can still hear her voice. "At once," she shouted. What a dressing-down they got for associating with us. The boy told me later on what his mother had said. He was also confined to the house for four days as a punishment. It didn't seem to bother him all the same. Both he and his sister continued to meet us whenever they could, but we were all careful to make sure that Madam never again got to hear of what was going on.

Another thing I couldn't understand at the time about the differences between us was why they got such long holidays from school — far longer than we had. They used to tell me about the schools they attended in England and I found it just as strange to hear that they went to different schools as they did to hear from me that in my school all the boys and girls were together sitting in the same classroom. This was something that amazed them both. They also used lots of words I had never encountered before and talked of things I had never heard about. One day I overheard them telling each other what they were going to get in their tuck boxes for the new term and it was ages before I realized what a tuck box was.

However, I learned a lot from them and in their own way I like to think that being so friendly with me taught them something too. Because, really, when we were all youngsters together neither side had much real idea of how the other side lived. They were as ignorant about the life of the working families on the estate as I was about what went on in their lives and how things were done in the Big House. They had absolutely no conception about what our life was like compared with theirs. None whatsoever. There was nothing unusual in this really, because in the 1930s few people knew much about anything outside their own class. Everyone stuck rigidly to his own class. As we saw it at the time it was like some barrier always there, always present, between us. On an estate there was no middle class. Only the upper class and the working class. As youngsters we didn't understand all the implications. We never gave much of a thought to the differences although without mentioning them we knew they were there.

It's the old, old story. Children, when left to themselves, have a way of breaking down stupid barriers such as those the laird's wife wanted to maintain. Everything is natural to a youngster. It was only the adults, especially the laird's wife, who insisted on trying to make life difficult for us. Yet, despite this, we all benefited as a result of our association. I know for my part, although I had no wish to work on an estate and didn't in fact work on one until after a career in the army, when I did come back to do a chauffeur's job, I had some idea of the laird's point of view and his problems. I might not always agree with him, but thanks to several years as a child spent in the company of youngsters from his class, then I was able to understand and make allowances from time to time when the going was rough.

When I eventually started on estate work I'd served in the army for twenty-two years and in addition to my driving experience I'd learned a bit about the mechanical side of vehicles. It wasn't enough to get me a job in a garage, but remembering my boyhood days on an estate I thought, well, I do know something about estate work. I could drive. I could do some light mechanical repair work. So I thought I'd try to combine both. I also realized that times had changed. The money paid to estate workers was a little better than in the days when my father had been slaving away for a mere pittance. There was also some sort of proper check on hours worked and, with some lairds, overtime was being paid for extra work done. Conditions had improved and anyway, as I now had a wife and three young children to look after, I couldn't afford to be too choosy. I decided to forget all the opinions I'd previously held about estate work and give it a try for myself. To take a chance. Luckily, I got a job straightaway as a chauffeur so I was able to carry on doing something I enjoyed — driving. I was also well used to ferrying people around in cars as one of my army jobs had been as driver to various senior officers.

I was a bit wary at first of doing this sort of thing in civilian life. Very wary, to tell the truth. I felt like a fish out of water, going back into an estate community. Despite my own

memories of an estate as a child I found lots of changes —
fewer people, tight control on the purse strings when it came
to the laird spending any money on improvements. And
whereas the pre-war chauffeur, like the one I'd seen with the
big Ford, would have been employed solely to drive and
maintain the vehicles, I was expected to do several other jobs
in addition to driving the laird and his family about the place
when required. This was all a bit bewildering at first. I was
very lonely.

I had a lorry to drive, carrying cattle and sheep to and from
the various markets. A great deal of fattening of cattle was
done on the estate farms — commercial beef is what it's
called — and transporting the fattened beasts away from the
place and bringing in the new ones was one of my main jobs.
I was also expected to do light mechanical repairs to the
estate vehicles, which included the laird's car, his wife's car,
the manager's car, the head gamekeeper's car, the
under-keeper's car, the shepherd's car and a Land Rover. I was
also in charge of a petrol tank and had to issue a supply of
petrol to all these people.

First thing every morning I had to go to the Big House and
stoke up the cooker, bring in a supply of coke and empty the
ashes so that all was ready for the cook to start work. I then
collected the milk pails and went to the Home Farm where
they were filled. When I'd delivered them back to the house it
was then time to clean the boots and shoes. Also in the
spring and summer I mowed all the lawns and grass alongside
the drives. At times it was a busy life, so much to do and not
enough time to do it all, when all the driving work had to be
fitted in as well.

On special occasions I had to put on my uniform when acting as chauffeur; if some important guest of the laird was being transported about or if the laird and his wife were attending a major function of some kind in the district. I didn't mind the dressing-up. In fact I quite enjoyed it really. I drove all sorts, the good and the bad.

The good ones would talk to you as if you were a normal human being, while the ill-mannered ones gave the impression that you were no better than dirt under their feet. They always sat in the back of the car and would never say a word to you throughout the length of the journey. This had the effect of making you feel really small, as if you were of no consequence whatsoever, just a mere servant. You soon got to know the real toff from the upstart. The real toff would say, "Can I sit in the front?" not "I'm going to sit in the front." He treated the car as if it were mine. There was politeness, a degree of respect, of courtesy. The upstart, he would climb into the back, I would shut the door, go round the front, get in, drive off and he would maintain a stony silence.

At first I found it uncomfortable and awkward to be driving someone who had no wish to speak, indeed who, you knew full well, would never speak because you just sensed they felt this would be beneath their dignity. Sometimes I might try to pass the time of day by asking if they had enjoyed their stay on the estate, fishing or shooting; or if I was bringing them to the Big House for a stay I'd remark about the prospects for the salmon fishing or the grouse or pheasant shooting. Small talk, but just enough to gauge the temperament of my passenger. The ones who sat in the front always seemed eager to talk. If they'd been to the estate before they'd be happy to recall previous visits and experiences or if they were coming for the first time they'd ask general questions about the layout of the place. The ones who sat in the back would only say "Yes" or "No" to your first questions so you just shut up and left them to themselves.

The longer I did the job the more amused I used to get by this haughty attitude, this image they presented of "I'm better than you and don't you forget it." At first it annoyed me, then later I just learned to have a good laugh about it. Anyhow it didn't do to let it worry you overmuch. I found the easiest thing was just to do my job and ignore them every bit as much as they chose to ignore me. Like every other job, you learned to accept that there would be pleasant times and bad times and that while most people, basically, were quite nice there were ones who, quite frankly, were only making themselves appear ignorant by their show of bad manners.

The laird himself, well, it took some time to get to know his ways. He always called me by my Christian name — John. But he called my wife Mrs John. I always resented this because, although it was an attempt on his part to be friendly, it wasn't really very nice. More patronizing really. Yes, it was familiar and easy-going, but on the other hand I'd have preferred it if he'd addressed my wife either as Mrs Jameson or even by her first name, just as he spoke to me. It should either have been one thing or the other instead of this forced familiarity which wasn't natural behaviour on his part.

I just treated the laird as I'd behaved towards my senior officers in the army. He had my polite respect, but no show of servility. It seemed to work. I knew as a result of my army experience what you could do and couldn't do and adopted the same attitude. It was by far the best way to tackle the job.

I found as a chauffeur it was easier to get along with the laird than with his wife. She was very much the upper-class lady. You were just the servant in her eyes and you were at her beck and call. She made this fact quite plain with her whole manner. I resented that. On a number of occasions it made me furious; really angry. I used to think to myself that if she'd only climb down from this high-minded posture she might be quite pleasant really. But she would persist in treating me as some sort of inferior being. Sometimes, if I was feeling charitable, I'd think she didn't realize what she was doing, but then due to some action or words you'd know full well that she enjoyed being the lady of the place and ordering around those who had to work for her.

On one occasion I was away from the estate all day driving beasts to market and when I got back I found my wife almost in tears. She told me she had been out at the baker's van when the laird's wife had turned up outside our house demanding petrol. The pump and tanks were just outside the main garage, which was beside our house. This was her standard way of doing things on most occasions — to make a demand. Just like some army officer issuing an order. And my wife had nothing to do with the issuing of petrol. That was my job. But as I was away from home quite a bit I always left the key in the house and those estate workers entitled to receive petrol could come and help themselves. What they got was recorded in a book. I trusted them and they trusted me. It was a good working relationship. Anyway, up comes her ladyship demanding petrol for her car and using her most officious voice. "I want petrol," she announced. My wife was still in the middle of doing her shopping from the van and said, "I'll be with you in just a minute." "I want petrol right away," says Madam. "I've no time to stand around here waiting for you."

This attitude really upset my wife and she gave her the keys in her own good time and let her get on with filling up the car with petrol. So when I heard about this when I got home I went off to the Big House in order to sort things out. I really went there to see the laird himself, but I bumped into her before I even reached the back door of the house. Straightaway I said, "I believe you had petrol today." She replied, "Yes, I had." I said, "Look here, my wife has got nothing to do with the issuing of petrol. That's my job." I could see she was angered by my own display of temper, riled at me daring to speak to her in such a way. She got quite haughty and said, "Oh but I wanted petrol and when I require it for my car I expect to get it." I said, "If you want petrol in future you tell me and not anybody else. It's no one else's business. Not even my wife's." She refused to say another word, just turned on her heels and stalked off.

I didn't manage to see the laird that evening so the next morning after I'd done all the chores, shoe cleaning, collecting milk and this sort of thing, the laird appeared in the passage and said he wanted to have a word with me. We went into a room and he tackled me immediately. "I believe you said something to my wife last night." Quite honestly I'd forgotten about the petrol incident by then. I'd been mad at the time, but having a row with her had got it out of my system and as is the usual way with me I just forgot about the entire thing. He went on to say something about her having said I'd been rude to her and I thought to myself that's just how she would present her side of the argument. She had always to be right. She always believed that she was right and everyone else was wrong. So I told him fully and quite bluntly what had happened and ended up by saying, "You put me in charge of the estate petrol. You gave me a key. And then you turn round and expect my wife to be at your beck and call on something that's got nothing to do with her. You're making a fool of me." I also knew by then that there was a second key floating about which his wife used to unlock the petrol pump as well as other members of his family. So I took my own key from my pocket and laid it on the table in front of him. I said, "There's my key and there's the petrol book. You can send somebody to dip the tanks. I'm having no more to do with it." I then just walked out and left him. I was fed up to the teeth with the whole petty business.

I carried on with my normal day's work. I think I had to go away for several hours to take sheep to one of the markets. Anyway, when I got home there were both sets of keys — my own and the one that had been in the laird's wife's possession. Seemingly the manager had been told by the laird what I'd said and done that morning and he had sorted it out. From that day on the petrol incident was never mentioned again and issues were made at a fixed time each day — by me alone.

This bit of trouble just showed me the value of sticking up for your rights. I've always believed in plain speaking and to a certain extent the laird was like this himself. He was usually able to see someone else's point of view if it was pointed out forcibly enough. Not always at first, but very often when he had been given sufficient time to think about it. His wife — never. For several weeks afterwards she remained very distant and more aloof than ever. I suppose in one way she just regarded the episode as yet another black mark against me in her book. But I wasn't bothered. The main thing was I had shown that I, as a working man, had every right to be treated with fairness and the laird in his own way had accepted the position without saying anything directly to me. This is the modern way of doing things on an estate. In my father's day — the bad old days as I like to think of them — if a worker had even dared to look rebellious or aggressive, never mind him saying anything in a fit of temper, he'd have been given his marching orders before he knew what was happening.

On another occasion I came home and found tools scattered around all over the garage floor. This made me furious because I always prided myself on keeping a tidy garage with everything in its proper place. I went into the house and immediately blamed my three sons. They said it had nothing to do with them and rather than argue about it I went back to tidy up the place. Just then the laird drew up in his car and straightaway got on to me for leaving the garage in such a mess. He was quite indignant. I remember him saying, "The tool box is the place for tools, not strewn about all over the place." As you can imagine this made me even more annoyed so I told him bluntly that I wasn't responsible, that none of my sons had anything to do with it and that this being so then the culprit must be one of his own sons. I'll be fair to him. He didn't argue with me. Just turned about and got into his car and went haring off along the drive to the Big House. Within twenty minutes or so he was back with his sons, one about eighteen, the other sixteen. In front of him the younger one admitted that he was responsible for the mess. He apologized and at once the laird, his father, told them both that in future they were not to use the garage for any repair work to their own vehicles without first asking me if they could. And they always did after that. There was no further animosity either from them or from me. As far as I was concerned the matter was settled and again it showed clearly the value of plain speaking.

That's the trouble with some people. Quite a few estate workers will just not point out any difficulties to their boss or complain if they feel they are being presumed upon. They'll merely grumble and moan among themselves. Mind you, there are always the ones who complain all the time and they're just as much of a nuisance to everyone else as they must be to the laird. But my laird was a forceful character himself so it required a certain amount of stubborn determination in order to handle his temperamental moments. He was a very obstinate man at times, especially when he had some fixed idea in his head.

As far as I am concerned the worst aspect of any estate job in Scotland is the perpetual sore point of the tied-house. It is a really bad thing. A man can give twenty, thirty or forty years of his life to an employer and be a faithful servant, but as soon as he falls by the wayside he's no more use and as a result not only is he likely to lose his job, but his house as well. I know exactly what happens as a result of my own experience.

I was taken sick and was told by my doctor that it would take a long time to get back to full fitness again. After the initial treatment in hospital I went back home. All I could do was sit around the house. It wasn't very pleasant, as you can well imagine, not just as a result of my illness, but because I have always been a person who likes to be out and about doing things, What I'm meaning is that it should have been fairly obvious to anyone who knew me that I couldn't be getting much enjoyment out of not working — and just appearing to be loafing around the place. But it certainly was not obvious to the laird. Altogether I was unfit to work for around eight months, but after about six weeks the laird was up in my house asking me if he could telephone the doctor to see when I would be ready to start work again. This annoyed me — the fact that despite the doctor's certificate which I'd submitted to him myself and the fact that I'd worked for him for over twelve years, he still refused to believe that there was anything substantially wrong with me. I just told him bluntly that this was a matter between the doctor and myself and that I'd no wish to shirk my work. He would just have to accept that. He didn't seem too pleased about my attitude and later, when I started to think about the conversation we'd had, I began to feel guilty. It started to prey on my mind.

Here I was, a man suffering from an illness, trying to recover and get fit again and he had made me feel bad as if I was in some way cheating him, my employer. I was made to feel humbled as a result of my predicament. And the more I thought about it the more I was able to reason. I was sitting in his house, doing nothing, living rent free (the rent and electricity being part of my wages) and although I couldn't help it there was no way I could stop myself wondering if he had already got hold of someone to do my job; and how soon would it be before I received my notice and the instructions to quit my house? So I had both the worry about my illness and the considerable guilt feelings about my whole position. It made me feel really insecure. And of course from the time he first raised the subject of telephoning my doctor, every time I saw the laird after that I was made to feel as if in some way I was letting him down, not pulling my weight, by being ill. It

90

may sound as if I was letting my imagination run riot, but believe me I was not. This constant nagging worry about the possibility of losing my house as a result of my illness was a very real and frightening situation, difficult to cope with. It hampered my recovery, I'm sure of this, and at the same time the laird was not much help by persistently giving the impression — intentionally or otherwise — that I was being a nuisance.

The situation got worse for me, month by month. The doctor's certificate was valid for a month at a time. I had to go to see him at the end of each month in order either to be signed-off or have the certificate renewed. It was three months before I was even allowed to drive my own car for short distances, but each time I was warned by the doctor that on no account could I do any heavy driving, such as with the lorry or as part of my chauffeur's duties. In the long run this began to make me very depressed. I expect one reason for this was the financial situation, but at least I was greatly helped here by my wife, who was going out to work and bringing in a wage to help keep the home going. So, really, the main cause of my depression was the continual nagging worry of living in a tied-house while unfit to work and knowing that sooner or later the laird was going to make a move to get me out of it and find someone else to take my place.

The biggest millstone around any estate worker's neck is the tied-house. A married man with a family such as myself is extremely vulnerable to all sorts of pressure. Too much is left to the goodwill of the individual laird as to what will be the fate of someone who falls ill for a long period and is occupying an estate house. You can be the best worker in the world, conscientious and giving a fair return for your wages, but the moment you fall ill, then that's when the crunch comes. If it's a long illness, such as mine was, then you just have to accept that eventually you will have to look for somewhere else to live. I would say, in the strongest possible terms — cut out the tied-house system, do away with it altogether. Some other system should be introduced where an estate worker pays a small rent for his house on a basis to be equal to the laird as well. This would mean that if a man fell ill then he would be protected by the rent he was paying from any premature eviction. Also, there should be some sort of agreement drawn up when he is first employed by the estate entitling him to, say, four months' or six months' notice of the laird requiring his house for another workman if he is no longer able to do the job he was employed to do. This would do away with the terrible situation of having your house as part of your wages, subject to only a month's notice before you're sent packing. I don't think it's a lot to ask in order to give justice to the estate worker in this respect. I expect, like many ideas intended to improve the lot of the workers, that the lairds would oppose it and put up all sorts of objections. The farmers certainly did in England when the government were in the process of passing a law doing away with tied-houses there for agricultural workers.

This may be a pet hate of mine, but then I know what I'm speaking about. I had to leave estate work because of it. I've been through all the worry and insecurity of a long illness while living in a house that goes with the job. It would be the best possible thing if tied-houses were done away with in Scotland. I really feel strongly about this. It was always a bone of contention. In the dim and distant past the situation was even worse, of course; you didn't have a month's notice to quit your tied-house then. Very often you had to be out by the next morning.

I can see the laird's point of view — to a certain extent. He obviously can't have all his houses occupied by workers unfit for their jobs. He must have some reasonable means of acquiring possession of them when one man gives up his job for whatever reason and he needs the place for the new man. But it needs a more humane approach, backed by the law. Having gone through some of the worst months of my life living with this threat of not only losing my job, but my home as well, it made me feel that I was trapped and absolutely in the power of my employer, dependent completely on whatever goodwill he thought fit to show to me. Nobody should be in this position nowadays — not in a so-called modern society.

It was the happiest day of my life when I received word from the local council that I had been allocated a council house in a nearby town. I was still off work and by now the laird seemed openly displeased and far from sympathetic. So, the day the letter arrived I never needed to think twice about the offer. I said to myself, "Well, that's it. That's me finished with estate work."

Now that I'm on the outside, as it were, I have no regrets at leaving estate work behind me. I feel a completely free man. I'm working again and have a boss. But my new boss has no hold on me in the same way that the laird had when I was his chauffeur. And although on the whole I enjoyed my years of work spent on an estate it's only now that I realize how independent I have become as a result of getting away from one. Many people who work on estates never give this a thought. They are content. Happily, most of them have no need to worry. But frankly, when I said goodbye to the estate it was like being given a new lease of life. The ways of a laird are not my ways. Good or bad, most lairds have too great a hold on the lives of those who work for them. In the past I never believed this was a good thing. Today, I think it's a situation in need of some radical changes, something completely at odds with the times.

CHAPTER
SEVEN

The magnificence of the red deer roaming the mountainous regions of Scotland is renowned throughout the world whether by people whose pleasure is in hunting them or merely observing and taking delight in the sight of creatures in their natural surroundings. A favourite subject in the paintings of Sir Edwin Landseer, there could have been few British homes in Victorian times without a copy of his *Monarch of the Glen* or *The Stag at Bay*, a classic stance showing the stag defiantly challenging the pursuing hounds.

On an estate such as Strathalder the deer have always been hunted, the traditional method being by stalking them across the open countryside. Any estate with access to extensive moorland values the existence of herds of red deer within its boundaries; like salmon fishing, pursuit of the deer is now not merely done for the sport and the pleasure, but as a means of providing a highly lucrative income from the rents provided by those who wish to test their skill against the cunning and instinct of a creature larger than any other on the estate, but more shy and nervous of approaching danger. However, despite the financial consideration — the rent from the hunter and the high price obtained from sale of the venison — stalking a deer is still regarded as one of the most difficult and exhilarating pursuits for those with an interest and love of field sports. Above all other methods of hunting it is the one that most closely follows the definition of "sport" laid down by Lord Walsingham, a prominent Victorian who wrote on all aspects of fishing and shooting. He maintained:

Sport may be defined as the fair, difficult, exciting, perhaps dangerous, pursuit of a wild animal, who has the odds in his favour, whose courage, strength, speed or cunning are more or less a match for or superior to our own, whose natural instinct engages a considerable amount of our intelligence to overcome it, and whose death, being of service, is justifiable.

Stalking deer most certainly contains all the elements of Lord Walsingharn's definition; and, as with fishing, if the estate is to make a success of it in attracting custom to its deer forest, then the employment of experienced stalking gillies is a first essential of good management. The head stalking gillie has an immense territory to watch over on Strathalder estate, several thousand acres of moorland, mountainside, ravines and gullies, patches of wind-blown pines in sheltered hollows. A deer forest need not contain any wood. In general terms it means an area of land cleared of sheep and cattle for the purpose of nurturing the deer. However, on some estates sheep do roam freely over parts of the land reserved for deer and when this happens the deer always move to the highest ground so as to be free from interference. On Strathalder the sheep are kept to the lowest parts of the moorland in order to give the red deer the space and the solitude in which they thrive best. The Strathalder deer forest is a model of its kind, the terrain being ideally suited for the purpose required of it; several high hills, rough and stony, for the stags, with plenty of good feeding for the hinds. There are also a number of large, open corries as well as numerous small ones, cutting into the slopes of the mountain where the deer can take shelter when caught in the open by a sudden gale. Several burns flow through the ground, providing a constant supply of drinking water and the isolated clumps of woodland provide a sanctuary for the beasts from the worst storms and a haven for the hinds when rearing their young.

Robert Graham, the head stalking gillie, finds it hard to say, even from his years of tramping the high ground of the estate, just how many deer are in the Strathalder herd. But he can always tell, within a reasonable margin for error, how many stags are around at any particular time of the year and how many hinds are suckling young. Being wild creatures, the deer are free to roam at will and could with little effort stray across the invisible boundary line and on to the land of the neighbouring estate. At times a part of the herd does this, but for most of the year and in particular during the short stalking season in the late autumn they remain within the heart of the deer forest, where conditions for their existence are at their best.

Although Robert Graham speaks of his herd it is not one herd in the conventional sense of the word as applied to domestic cattle; there may be a total of seven or eight hundred deer of all ages on the estate grouped in four, perhaps five, herds of varying numbers, each with its leader, a stag of greater physical power and presence than any of his rivals.

Robert Graham is a man who has seen the wildest and most isolated corners of the Strathalder estate and who, despite the familiarity born of experience and constant contact, still manages to achieve total harmony with the immense tract of landscape which he moves through, silent and observing, on almost every day of the year.

Even without firing a shot at a beast nothing could be more enjoyable than climbing the hills in the early morning, watching the quiet herds taking up their position for the day just between the winds. You can lie there in the heather and watch the little ones playing, scampering about, kicking their hind legs in the air, while the older deer are perhaps wallowing in a mud bath where there is boggy ground near to a burn. One or two of the old hinds will be to one side on sentry duty. Then, as you sit and watch, spying on them through your telescope, trying to count the heads, spot the best heads among them, the sun will be starting to warm you and you are aware of nothing in the world except the sight of those creatures and the sounds of the upland birds, a raven croaking, a grouse chattering in a hollow; perhaps, if you're lucky, the echoing call of an eagle perched on the very top of a nearby crag. No matter how down-hearted I might be about some mundane problem at home, once I get up on to the mountain, once I get into the heart of the place where the deer are, all my worries fade away. They cease to exist in such surroundings. It's the most wonderful place in the world to me.

I started my working life as a kennel boy on the estate, looking after the dogs, feeding them, cleaning the kennels, washing and scrubbing the larders, skinning deer and all that sort of thing. After about a year there was a vacancy for a gamekeeper and I got the job. I lived in the bothy along with three other single men. We did our own cooking, took turn about doing that — all very elementary, basic stuff, pretty rustic. All in all we generally fended for ourselves.

During the course of the year, apart from looking after a beat on the moor, keeping down vermin and predators in search of the grouse, I became stalking gillie to one of the estate deerstalkers. Now, as a gillie I had an important part to play in the stalking team. The stalker of the beat did all the actual stalking of the deer. He carried the rifle, took the guest right in to the beast, sometimes over miles of difficult terrain, then handed over the rifle for him to take a shot at it. The guest then took his shot at the stag and either hit it or missed, according to how good an eye he had. As the gillie, I went with the stalking party and carried the lunch bag; and when the stag was killed I had to bleed it by cutting its throat (gralloching is what we call this) then go and make contact with the ponyman and help him to load the beast on to the pony's back.

When we returned to the Big House in the evening we all had to muck-in and skin the deer. The skull head was always placed to one side. At the end of the week it was my job to

100

gather up all the heads that had been skulled and boil the flesh off them, ready for the guests who had been out stalking to take their trophies away with them when they departed at the weekend. Some left them behind for the laird to mount and hang if he wished, but they usually took them away. Each guest was allowed at least one good trophy head and the main thing was to keep up the standard of the stags in the deer forest by killing out all the deer with narrow heads and leave the big stags with the wide heads. Royals and Imperials, they weren't touched, except for special guests whom the laird respected as being first-rate shots and who would appreciate the magnificence of owning such a splendid trophy.

A Royal is a stag with twelve points on his antlers — that's six points on each horn — and an Imperial has seven points on each horn. With fourteen points on a splendid head he really is an awe-inspiring beast when you see him through a telescope, perhaps standing there on the fringe of a herd scattered along a ridge against the skyline.

The stalking and shooting of stags can usually start about the end of August. They've got clear of their "velvet" by then (the soft growth which protects their newly-emerging horns, which are freshly grown each year). By then the horns have turned brown and become hard. It is then possible to stalk right through to around the 20th of October, but on most estates it stops around the 10th because the rutting season is starting to get underway. The stags start to roar, challenging other males to fight, and seeking mates. What a fantastic sound it is — this roaring. To anyone hearing it for the first time it can be quite frightening and unless you know what you're doing it's best to keep out of the way of the stags when they are in this state. When rutting begins the blood becomes impure. If you skin a stag during or near the rutting season your hands, indeed any part of your skin that the hands have touched, erupt in small festering sores. It's very painful and highly contagious.

Of course in the old days, both before and for many years after the Second World War, things were totally different in the stalking fraternity. There was absolutely no commercialism involved then. It was all sheer sport, pure and simple. Friends and acquaintances of the laird would be invited to take part in what was, in effect, a shooting holiday. They were here on the estate by his direct invitation and the majority were dedicated shots with a keen eye and a willingness to participate in every aspect of the stalk. By this, I mean the actual shooting of the beast is only the climax to the whole complex operation, which might start several hours previously; hard, difficult, uncomfortable travel over miles of territory in order to get into a suitable position to make the shot. Most of the old-timers revelled as much in this side of things as they did in the firing of the actual shot which brought down the beast. Nowadays, those taking part in stalking pay large sums of money for the sport and, unhappily, many of them seem totally uninterested in anything except the killing or how many beasts they can take in order to recoup some of the expenditure involved.

In the past there was no market for the meat. The beasts would be skinned and the venison distributed to the estate workers or to anyone living on estate property, retired workers, tenant farmers. In the early 1930s — between 1930 and 1932 — when the Depression was at its height and some places, particularly the mining areas, were extremely badly hit, living in poverty and nearly at the point of starvation, the deer were skinned and the carcases despatched to the most badly affected areas of Britain. So that was one outlet and a thoroughly deserving one. However, in the main, at all times the meat was simply divided between Big House and employees. A completely different state of affairs exists today.

The game dealers will now buy the stags complete with heads, feet and skins — the lot — and pay on average around 56p a pound gross weight for each beast. An average stag weighs around twelve stones so is worth over £90; quite a good return, all said and done. It was after the Second World War when the commercial side of deer stalking began to make itself felt, in the early 1950s, but by around 1970 there was a considerable market for venison, something that has existed and increased ever since because of the demand and the changed relationship with Germany and other Continental countries. They are the main source of demand for venison and practically all the meat goes over there now for game soup and all this sort of thing.

A stalk begins with the stalker spying out with his telescope all the slopes and ridges along the mountain range. You will probably see one or two stags loitering near the hinds because after the end of August there is a tendency for the male beasts to break away from the main segregated groups that have lasted throughout the winter, spring and summer. You'll pick out a parcel of deer and there may be one or two good stags and a few poor stags hanging about. So you select your group of deer and you watch the wind. You might have to do a four- or a five-mile detour to get into position in order to come up-wind to your beasts. Now, the trouble always is with hinds, especially the older hinds — they are far more alert than the stags. There are always two or three on the outskirts of each herd who appear to be the sentinels, the watchers. They are the ones you have got to pay the greatest heed to. You size up the lie of the land; there might be ridges, there may be a ditch or a burn with high banks; and you plan your stalk, which will take you as close as possible to the target you will select.

Now, invariably, at some stage you will come to an open piece of ground that you've simply got to cross before you can get really close to your deer. So, you have the muzzle of the rifle covered over and you set off crawling flat on your belly. If possible, you try to pick long heather to go through and you're scraping and slithering along getting scratched by the heather stalks and bitten by the dozens of insects that always seem to be around in such a place on a hot day. But you've just got to ignore all the discomforts. You might have to go through marsh and bog land. I've had water running down from my neck and my clothing absolutely soaked. But you take no notice because all the while your eyes are on that group of deer you're attempting to reach. No matter how seasoned and hard-bitten a stalker you are, you still feel your heart beating wildly at this stage in the proceedings. There is always the feeling of excitement. In the open you are at your most vulnerable and being exposed like this means you must call on every reserve of knowledge and skill you possess in order to cross the open ground and reach some shelter. That's what I love about stalking. It's a complete battle of wits, pitting your experience against a highly nervous animal, alert to every possible danger, ready to flee at the slightest hint of trouble.

104

Anyhow, you get in to a point where you are either close enough for a reasonable shot or it's impossible to get any further because you would be in full view of all the herd. You must then get your rifle forward; get yourself a little mound to rest it on because you can't get up on your elbows otherwise too much of your body will be showing against the background. You select the stag. If you're stalking on your own as part of your job you always select the poor heads (the good ones are left for the guests) and depending on the location you decide whether to go for one beast or a couple. If you're alone and the ground is difficult territory you'll only want one if you have to drag it a long way to the nearest track or point where a pony or Land Rover can reach it. However, if the pony can be brought in comfortably you might take two, perhaps three, providing you're able to get clean shots at them all.

The object of the exercise is to place the rifle bullet in the heart or some other vital part that will ensure a swift death — right there on the spot. The great secret is to know exactly how and when to take your shot. Some people want to fire at too great a distance, some are anxious to get too near. Deciding how best to do it is something that comes to you easily after a good deal of experience. A good rule is: up to eighty yards away from the beast is usually close enough. If you're two hundred yards or more away then you should never fire. So you take aim, then fire. Hopefully, the beast drops dead instantly.

The next job is to bleed it by cutting the throat. The blade of the knife actually goes right down to the heart — you sever the main artery — otherwise the flesh will be tainted and will not keep for any length of time. The stalk is over. Your job is done. Well, that's not strictly true, because you then have to deal with getting the beast away from where it lies and manhandle it to a point where transport can collect it to take it back to the estate premises. It's hard work on a boiling hot day. But the exhilarating part of it is over, the stalk itself, when throughout the whole time you've been making your approach never once have you thought of it as being hard work. No matter how experienced you are there is always the thrill of the stalk present within you.

Stalking on your own, keeping an eye on the herds and culling the poorer beasts is, to some people's way of thinking, a lonely life. You're away out on the mountains all day long with not even a dog for company, but, you know, never once have I found it unpleasant not to have anyone to speak to — to do my day's work alone. The surroundings provide you with so much interest and variety that the day passes without your even noticing the time go by. Of course, a stalk itself might take several hours to accomplish, but when you are not intent on getting a shot at a beast you'll be aware of all the wildlife around you; curlews, plovers, ravens, to name but a few of the species of upland birds. And there's the animals, wildcats, a fox, perhaps a sight of a vixen hunting for food for her cubs. And while on the face of it moorland and mountain may appear silent and desolate terrain, there are constant sounds attracting your attention; the calling of grouse, or higher up, the secretive ptarmigan, a dog fox barking, the bleating of sheep far off in some distant fold in the land. No, there are plenty of worthwhile things to see and hear out on the hill. And if I had to make a choice I think I'd far rather go out stalking on my own than be with a guest no matter how much of a sportsman he might be.

106

To be a good deer stalker, someone who feels completely at home in isolated surroundings, it's important to be a person in possession of a solitary soul. Something inside of you craves for solitude. Your nature and temperament must either adapt and mould itself to the nature of your surroundings or, if it doesn't and the lonely life is having a bad effect on you, it's time to find some other job. Quite often the stalking gillie lives in the most remote part of the estate — the house being practically among the mountains. This may be good for the man, to be so close to the territory for which he is responsible, but for his wife it can often be a trying time while she adjusts herself to being so far from shops, neighbours and what would probably be called — though wrongly in my opinion — civilized society. Nowadays, with Land Rovers and good hill tracks to run them on, it's possible for the stalker to live closer to the hub of the estate. Within thirty minutes or so in the Land Rover and he can be on his beat with ease. This has made a substantial difference to our way of life. But not always for the better, in my opinion. Living in the heart of the estate means you get involved with all the day-to-day happenings and if you're not careful it's possible to find yourself on one side or the other in any dispute, often in matters which don't really concern you. You're too close to estate politics. Up there — on the moor, away from it all — you're your own man; a free agent. You can come and go as you please and there's no one to bother you. And, naturally, if you want some company you can go off and find some, rather than having it forced on you all the time, often when you're not in the mood for it.

Now, if you're a bit of a lone individual — like me — you have to be extremely careful in acting diplomatically with

107

some of the paying guests. Firstly, you must realize that this fellow has paid through the nose for his sport. To him there is only one object. To stalk and kill the most magnificent beast he can get a hold of. He may be a thoroughly decent individual, generous and courteous, or he may be the most self-centred, arrogant swine you've ever set eyes on. Nevertheless, they must be treated alike, given the same consideration, given the benefit of every bit of experience you have in order to allow them to achieve their ambition. This is the hardest part of my job; being nice and polite when, in reality, I'd dearly love to give them a piece of my mind. However, there are compensations. One thing about deer stalking is that you develop a good sense of patience. You have to be patient in this job because it's not something that can be accomplished in five minutes. So, you put this long-suffering patience of yours to good use and this allows you to deal with the awkward customers in an orderly, reasonable fashion. They don't deserve it, mind you. But you've got to do it this way.

It's the easiest thing in the world to lose your temper with someone who cannot crawl over open ground or who, knowing the importance and delicacy of such an operation, starts talking or complaining about the discomforts right in the middle of it. Another troublesome character is the person who will insist on poking up his head to have a look to see where the beasts are. A stalker, if he's got to look, raises his head very slowly so that there's no quick break in the background, no sudden silhouette appearing above the line of the normal surroundings. Deer are extremely sharp and quick to spot hasty or unusual movements against the background or on the skyline. You'll get deer looking absolutely straight at you, but if you keep your head down and lie motionless their curiosity will disappear. They'll go back to their grazing or whatever they're up to. It's the sudden movement they spot and the inexperienced person — or the stupid one — will usually jerk his head up to see what's going on. Quick as a flash the deer detect the movement and they're off. If this happens you can bet your life that when they do settle down again some distance away it will be doubly hard to get near them. They will be extremely suspicious.

You can forgive a person for doing this once if he doesn't appreciate the seriousness of it; you can forgive him a second time if he forgets your advice. But on the third occasion it happens, despite your polite instructions to the contrary, then it's all you can do to stop yourself from blasting off. Of course you can't, beyond pointing out yet again the error of their ways. Sometimes I'd like to tell this type of guest exactly what I think of them — the selfish, inconsiderate ones. To do this would make me feel really good inside. But it's they who dictate the terms now. They're just as much your boss as the laird, even although they may have only taken the stalking for a brief period. They are the new élite. Once upon a time some of them would never have been allowed near a rifle or a stag. But now it's different. Times have changed. Money talks. And they have plenty of both. In a strange sort of way it's just as well they have come on the scene. It's the money from the new rich that's keeping many estates going today — it's keeping them afloat. Money from renting grouse shooting, salmon fishing and deer stalking. So who am I to complain? If it wasn't for them I might not even have a job now. They're giving me the opportunity to go on living the way I want to live, do the job I really like, be in the only place I ever want to be. I suppose I should be grateful.

In the old days there was always a flask of whisky carried by the stalking team — stalker, guest, gillie, ponyman. Of course it belonged to the guest and the ponyman looked after it, along with the guest's lunchbag slung over the pony's back. So there was a good old stiff drink all round after a stalk had been successfully accomplished and the stag killed. Then, when you got back to the larder he would be off to the Big House and if he was particularly proud of the beast he'd shot or perhaps the way he'd shot it, he would return with his wife or the laird in order to admire the beast. There was great elation over a good head and we all shared in the guest's jubilation. Whisky flowed freely and so, too, did the tips. Money was no object to some. But it wasn't given to you in any patronizing fashion or grudgingly because it was the done thing to tip. Oh no. It was handed over as a mark of respect for the manner in which I'd led the stalk and to reward the gillie and ponyman's hard work in bringing the body back down off the hill.

Some of the old-style guests became good friends of mine whether they were "Sirs" or "Lords" or what have you. Class or rank never entered the matter. It was respect and trust in each other that was at the root of it all. This dictated the strength of the relationship. They knew I could do my job. I could give them that trophy at the end of the day if they followed my instructions. The good ones made life easy by learning fast if they'd never been on a stalk before. The bad ones — well, they just soldiered on making the best of a bad job, never satisfied and never able to see the reason why. I expect they were like that in other parts of their lives.

110

In the early 1930s a terrible thing happened to the red deer, not only on this estate but in several other major forests in Scotland. There was a plague of ticks, blood-sucking insects that infest long heather and bracken. The deer were blamed for spreading it among the sheep population. So the order went out to the stalkers: kill the deer. As many as you possibly can. The sheep were being badly affected and many of them were dying. The estate was losing dozens of them, right, left and centre; all over the place. At that time the deer were of no value whereas sheep were, providing a considerable income from the fleeces and the mutton. We spent two years slaughtering the deer. We killed hundreds of fine beasts — stags and hinds. And apart from the carcases taken in to be skinned and sent to the depressed mining areas, the rest, the vast majority I might say, were just left lying there in the open out on the hills. Left to the eagles to feed on and the foxes and the crows.

It was a time of considerable sadness for me because I hate seeing any animal killed indiscriminately. And this was wholesale slaughter. There's no other way to describe it. There was no sport in it. Good, healthy deer and poor, stunted creatures — they all perished the same way. And the irony was that several years after all this killing some scientists looked into the phenomenon and there were very grave doubts as to whether the deer had actually been the tick-carriers. It appeared that the killing had been almost totally unnecessary as the ticks could just as easily have been spread among the sheep by grouse or foxes or any other of the wild creatures inhabiting the uplands. Of course, the estate was denuded of deer and it took many years to get stocks up to a reasonable level again. I doubt very much if such a thing

111

could happen today. Deer are too valuable now with this terrific demand for venison and high prices being paid for the carcases. There's a definite change of policy now on the estate. Deer are really worth far more than sheep and any estate with ideal upland ground, like this one, will go right out and encourage the deer to stay around. Full-scale stalking is going strong again.

Deer stalking was always looked upon as "the" thing. It still is, to a certain extent, by some of the sporting fraternity. It was the highlight of the sporting year. If a man shot two hundred brace of grouse he'd be less proud of that achievement than by getting a Royal stag. There is the

element of skill to consider and that of being hardy. You've got to be hardy in order to succeed. Your terrain is rough and to achieve success you have to really work hard at it. The first thing to consider is that you're hunting a noble creature, perhaps the most noble of all Britain's wild animals. Secondly, your trophy of the beast's head can be kept forever, handed down throughout generations. It's a different matter with the shooting of small game, grouse, pheasants and partridges. They just become figures in a book. You have nothing more than this to show for your success — nothing at all after the memory of the particular day has faded. But with a stag — a good stag's head you can keep. It's indestructible. You don't have to remember the day you shot it and what it was like as a beast. Its magnificent head is there on display for all time. For all to see. To a sportsman that means a great deal.

CHAPTER
EIGHT

Strathalder House stands in a narrow glen, surrounded by trees and facing the river. While still an imposing building when viewed amid such a glorious setting, as a building of architectural merit it is now no more than a shadow of its former self. Like so much connected with the estate and its spacious grounds the glory of the house belongs to the past, to another age.

Much of the old house has been demolished, it having been too large and cumbersome to maintain. Built originally in 1867 when Strathalder estate was formed (one of three estates to take possession of land being sold off from an estate which had existed in the area for several centuries) the original house was of granite; a granite pile, facing south, with numerous turrets, crow-stepped gables and enormous windows, those in the turrets being of curved glass. Entrance was made through an imposing tiled porch and massive doorway into a vast hall dominated by an equally impressive and gigantic fireplace and paintings of Highland scenes hanging on every wall. In the hall and the dining room there was oak panelling from floor to ceiling. All the rooms were spacious; study, morning room, breakfast room, drawing room, this having as its

focal point an elegant marble fireplace of greater proportions and more intricate design than any other room in the house. A crystal chandelier hung from an ornate plaster rosette in the centre of the ceiling. The library was lined with dark, sombre bookcases full of volumes of all sorts and in the centre of the considerable floor area was a large, leather-topped table with drawers; huge leather armchairs were placed at strategic points around the room. The billard room was across the corridor and at the back and on two levels, ground floor and basement, the kitchen, scullery, cellar, store rooms and the servants' sitting room and dining room.

On the upstairs levels the rooms on the south side of the house, with their views towards the river, the wooded slopes and the moorland beyond, were all bedrooms — brass bedsteads, big mirrors on the dressing tables, large chests of drawers — the master bedrooms with dressing rooms attached and splendid bathrooms, gothic in taste with six-foot long baths with brass taps and wooden loo mounted on a throne. A corridor ran from end to end and on the north side were the servants' servicing rooms and various cubby-holes; linen rooms, broom cupboards, rooms for making tea when large parties of guests were being entertained in the house. On the floor under the eaves, where the rooms had sloping ceilings, was the nursery, close to the schoolroom, quarters for the nanny and the governess and bedrooms for the children. A back staircase gave access to the servants' sleeping quarters on the same level.

Every single thing was designed on a massive scale requiring a regiment of servants to look after it, together with infinite finance to see to the upkeep of the structure of so vast a building. The original house remained intact long after the first signs of change had made themselves apparent, initially in the 1930s, then, more forcibly, during the years of the Second World War. During this time there were fewer servants than in previous years, but a successful attempt was made, despite the diminishing numbers, to ensure that standards were maintained; life went on within its walls in very much the same fashion as before. Post-war Britain put a finish to that; by the early 1950s expense and the difficulty of finding staff willing to live-in, as their predecessors had done, forced the laird and his wife to close off much of the house and to retreat to living quarters in one wing of the building. The sight of the empty, decaying shell of the remainder of the house continued to haunt them and plans were soon made for the partial demolition and renovation of the structure. With this now complete, Strathalder House in its modern guise occupies only a modest proportion of the area once filled by its Victorian counterpart.

A part of the old building remains (there are still a couple of turrets) but inside the rooms are considerably fewer — and smaller. The house retains a form of elegance while, at the same time, managing to generate the atmosphere of a family home — a lived-in place with dogs on the hearth and paintings on the walls, unostentatious, yet clearly the house of a country gentleman and his wife. There are now no resident servants; what work has to be done is taken care of by the laird's wife herself and a number of estate workers' wives who assist on a part-time basis with cooking and cleaning as required. No butler prowls the dining room, no resident cook controls her kitchen and her staff with as much firmness and discipline as that once wielded by the lady of the house herself. Like the old house they, too, are but memories from the past.

Jessie Gordon worked on a number of estates in a variety of capacities as a member of the kitchen staff — scullery maid to cook. She recalls that from the end of the First World War in 1918 through to the late 1920s the working day was long and in her kitchen followed a rigid timetable of events in order to ensure that every job was done — and done well. At the time there was a kitchen staff of four; head cook, under-cook, kitchen maid and scullery maid.

The scullery maid and the kitchen maid had to rise at 4.45 every morning and come down to clean the two monstrous ranges in the kitchen; flue them, blacklead them, polish until all the right bits shone, scour every single one of the steel parts with emery paper.

They had to be cleaned, just as if they had never seen a day's use and were, in fact, brand new. What a palaver. Then there were the racks on top for keeping things hot. They'd all to be polished as well — they were steel. And around the walls, on shelves, were all the steel covers for placing on top of plates and ashets to keep the food warm; they had to be cleaned once a week. And all this had to be done before the cook arrived down at 7.30 a.m.

The scullery maid had then to go and wash the long passage from the servants' dining hall, right to the back door. Wash it out every morning or scrub it thoroughly if it had become too dirty; also apply pipe-clay about a foot distance in from each wall — white pipe-clay to make the surrounds look like a border.

And the kitchen maid, by this time, of course, she was busy getting things organized for the cook, putting out oatmeal and so forth for the making of the porridge, getting the pot on the fire to get it to come to the boil and her frying pans all put out on top of the range, each one upside down to heat the inside thoroughly. Having seen to all this she would then have to get started on baking the morning scones. There were scones baked every morning — what they called the morning scone roll. They were done on a plate. The dough, once mixed, had to be put into the ovens and cooked. All this had to be ready as well by the time the cook came down at 7.30a.m. Everything had to be finished when the cook made her appearance at 7.30a.m. Every single thing.

The breakfast was at eight o'clock for the staff. Breakfast for the gentry upstairs was at nine o'clock. The kitchen maid always had the job of getting the breakfast ready for the staff. She was allowed to cook it because it didn't really matter what happened to it — within reason, of course. But the cook took over control to see to the upstairs breakfast. Nothing must ever go wrong with it. The staff breakfast was porridge and milk and the rolls — the scone rolls — any of those that were maybe overcooked, slightly brown, they were put through to feed the staff, along with a big pot of tea. And that was that. The staff had their own dining room and they all gathered there for their breakfast. It was the scullery maid's

119

job to clear the table, to take the dishes back to the kitchen, wash them, dry them and stack them back into their proper places. There wasn't much time for dallying over your breakfast because everyone had to be ready in good time to see to the breakfast upstairs.

The food was sent up on a pull-lift — a dumb waiter — and the butler or one of the young footmen was waiting there to take it off. The meal was served at table, dead on the stroke of nine o'clock. Every day without fail. The laird was a stickler for punctuality, not only among his staff, but from his own family as well. Even his guests were expected to conform. The food was never kept hot to await the appearance of anyone who might have overslept or been delayed for however innocent a reason. Nine o'clock was breakfast time and if you weren't there on time, then that was just too bad. Your food got cold and you had only yourself to blame. That's the way the laird looked at it when it came to every meal of the day, breakfast, lunch and dinner. In a way his attitude was a great help to the staff, both in the kitchen and serving in the dining room. Everyone knew exactly what was happening and when it was happening. And the cook's efforts in preparing a worthwhile meal were rewarded because she would have it ready in time, as was part of her job, and those folks who were going to sit down and eat it were there, too, ready to enjoy it. Many's the story I've heard of rows starting and cooks leaving to work in other country houses because there were so many last-minute changes in the meal routines. And other staff, too, who might find themselves working even longer than they were expected to do just to suit the whims and fancies of the laird or his family and guests. They found it hard to put up with such fiddling about. The job was difficult

— and arduous — enough as it was. But that never happened here. We were all glad of it. It made for a happier working relationship among us all. Meal-times were meal-times and everyone stuck rigidly to the rules.

Most of the gentry ate porridge in the morning and probably kidney and sausage, bacon and egg; maybe fish. During the fishing season this fish at breakfast time might have been trout — even a sea trout. Delicious. And coffee at one end of the table; tea at the other.

When their breakfast was finished and all the dishes had been brought back to the kitchen again, it was time for the scullery maid to get weaving once more — and wash and dry all this lot. Sometimes, if there were lots of guests and extra plates to see to, the kitchen maid would lend a hand. While they were getting on with this job the lady of the house would come down about ten o'clock to give the cook her orders as to what meal should be prepared for lunch, at 1p.m.; how many were to be there to eat it, and what she wanted for dinner at 8.15 in the evening.

And mind you, that was the kitchen staff — the maids at least — up at 4.45 in the morning, the dinner was at 8.15 at night and very often the gentry were never out of the dining room until after 10.30. And there was still washing up to be done, with the kitchen maids waiting about to do it. So it was a long hard slog, I can tell you, working in the kitchens. Wearying work for precious little money. The scullery maid had ten shillings a week plus her meals and board and her uniform; the kitchen maid was getting fifteen shillings and the cook had £1.10s for her week's work. Long hours, very long hours and even compared with some other jobs not particularly good wages to compensate you for all this toil.

121

But those who worked in the kitchens were almost always women who felt they were part of a long tradition of service. A girl usually started because her mother had been in service and most girls had the ambition of ending up as a cook. This was the key job in the kitchen, of course. She was boss. It was her kitchen, not her ladyship's. If you worked in the kitchen it didn't really matter too much what sort of person was the lady of the house. If you were a lowly worker you very rarely ever came into contact with her, except to nod and say "Good-day." It was the personality and nature of the cook you had to worry about. If you worked with a good cook, not just someone who could cook well, I mean, but somebody who was fair, kind-hearted and generous — no, that's not the word — compassionate, in her dealings with the rest of the kitchen staff under her control and was willing to patiently teach the younger girls, help them to learn to do the job properly, then you felt you had landed-up in Heaven. But if you found yourself with a tyrant — and by God there were plenty of this kind around — bad natured, overbearing, officious, then it seemed as if you had gone to the other place. Your life became a misery and you spent every free moment dreaming of escape to get away to another household where the atmosphere was better.

Our cook, I'm pleased to say, was one of the former kind — strict, but very fair. And she was always one for a laugh and a joke when there were free moments, lulls in the general hustle and bustle of the day.

Sometimes her ladyship's instructions were quite simple; at other times, if a full-scale dinner party was being planned, the orders were fairly elaborate. She had a great eye for detail did her ladyship. Yet so, too, had the cook. So they suited each

122

other. The average lunch would be a four or five course affair followed by coffee with, when the season was right, lots of fruit. It was similar at dinner with the addition of a fish course in between the soup and the meat. They'd start off with soup, broth perhaps, then the fish course, often a salmon or sea trout made up into a pâté, with a salad; then meat. In the game season this would be grouse or pheasant, but usually it was meat of some kind; there was always roe deer hanging in the game larder. But it could just be roast beef or pork, something of this kind. The puddings were quite plain really, when you see some of the fancy dishes people are always talking about today. In the fruit season it would be fresh fruit and cream and in the winter lots of steamed puddings and caramel puddings. The laird was known for his sweet tooth and the cook saw to it that he was well looked after in this direction. Coffee finished the meal. Always coffee. It was served in the drawing room, of course. The company split up at this stage. The gents were left to their glass of port and the ladies went through for their coffee. After half an hour or so they all got together again in the drawing room where they usually played cards for an hour before finishing off, ready for bed. A very leisurely life. While downstairs all the plates were being washed and stacked and the kitchen staff were looking forward to a cup of tea or cocoa and a sandwich or a biscuit before going off to their beds; ready for the next day when the whole thing would begin all over again in exactly the same fashion.

In the mornings, after her ladyship had finished talking to the cook she went back upstairs and the kitchen maid was called in to see the cook. She was told about all the different vegetables that had to be got ready for lunch and all the various vegetables needed for dinner in the evening. All the vegetables had to be cleaned and prepared by the kitchen maid. That was her job. And then she would be told if she had any wafers or things of this kind to make for serving with the soup. It was the kitchen maid's responsibility to see to the making of them. This meant that the cook was then free to concentrate on her cooking and baking for the rest of the day.

There was always plenty of baking being done. The ladies of the house, especially if there were guests staying, would have afternoon tea around 4p.m. So the cook had to see to it that they were well supplied with lots of home-made scones and cakes. I can still get the smell of that kitchen when baking was in progress — the scent of the pastry, the delicious smells wafting from the ovens as the scones and cakes, tray upon tray of them, were baked to absolute perfection. Lovely. Absolutely the loveliest memory I have of my time in the kitchen of that enormous house.

At around 10.15 every morning one of the gardeners would arrive in the kitchen — usually one of the foremen or journeymen — to get his orders for vegetables from the cook. By this time, having seen the lady of the house, the cook would have prepared a list of her requirements for the day's meals. There was usually a store of potatoes in the house, so on the list would be such things as spinach, carrots, celery, leeks, peas or beans — all the different vegetables available in the estate garden, but a good variety so that there would be different vegetables served at dinner than were on the menu for lunch. So, he got his instructions from the cook and, if he was on good terms with her, he was favoured with a cup of tea and one of her cakes. After this, off he went to the head gardener to pass on the request from the cook.

The head gardener, being a man who knew every inch of his garden and no doubt the condition of most of the plants, could then tell him where to go to get the best vegetables, to select the ones in the finest condition. The orders were then passed along the line of command — the journeyman instructing one or two of the gardeners to set about picking the peas or lifting the carrots or leeks, whatever jobs had to be done. Once this was completed the consignment would, most likely, be shown to the head gardener for his approval. And before the load was taken back to the house to the cook, every single vegetable had to be washed thoroughly so that not a trace of earth remained on the roots or the leaves. Carrots had to be washed, leeks had to be washed. And if the gardeners wanted to keep on the right side of the cook then they made sure that the job was done to perfection.

The gardener brought the vegetables to the kitchen in a barrow or sometimes, if the house was full of guests and the order was very big, it would arrive in a little cart drawn by a pony. The first thing the cook would do was inspect the vegetables, run her sharp eyes over the lot and anything that wasn't up to her standards, either because it was dirty or bruised, was rejected. It went back straightaway, without comment, and fresh substitutes were brought without delay. This didn't happen very often, of course, because great care was taken.

But I do remember one occasion when practically the whole barrow load was sent back. And it wasn't the gardener's fault. The daughter of the house had just received a bicycle as a birthday present. Naturally, she spent a lot of her time careering around the drives on this bike, going at great speeds, not a thought in her head of danger or the chance she'd ever have an accident. Well, she was haring along the drive between the house and the gardens when, on a sharp corner, she met the journeyman wheeling his barrow. She went straight into it and capsized barrow and contents, escaping herself except for a graze on her knees. Tomatoes, carrots, leeks, everything was scattered all over the gravel and as a result got into a bit of a mess. The gardener and she gathered them up as best they could and put them back in the barrow, but when they eventually reached the cook it was quite obvious to her that some disaster had happened on the way. Quite a lot of things were marked and bruised, tomatoes burst. He explained to the cook, but she was quite firm. Most of it would have to go back. And it did. The cook's word was law. All the same I'm sure there were a few swear words flying around in the gardens that morning before the whole thing was sorted out and the fresh supply of vegetables obtained.

By now, then, in the kitchen it would be about 11.30a.m. and the kitchen maid got busy preparing the vegetables selected for the lunch, cleaning and dressing them, while the cook, in addition to preparing the lunch, would be here, there and everywhere making sure all was going according to plan.

Agnes Black was a kitchen maid and at times found the rigid routine of each long, hard day extremely monotonous. The discipline also tended to get on her nerves, but despite this she saw no reason to blame the cook for keeping such strict control over her staff.

The cook reigned supreme in her own kitchen. She was boss. Discipline was her first concern — then cleanliness. She was so obsessed by this that she even made sure her own staff were properly dressed before she'd allow them to go for their meals with the other household staff in our own dining room.

In the mornings, as a kitchen maid, I had to wear a pale green linen frock with a green apron, while the cook was dressed in a black frock and white apron with hat. Now, before I was able to go to the dining room to have my breakfast the cook would inspect me as if I was a soldier on parade, checking that my dress was clean and all looked neat and respectable. Of course the others were subjected to the same treatment. We never objected. Well, we couldn't — could we? We'd have been out on our ears looking for another job if we had. And anyway it was just a part of that way of life. Something you expected to happen to you. All the same, I was only about twenty and thought it a bit of a laugh, but one of the other kitchen maids we had was in her mid-thirties. Later, when I left and got married I did wonder what she thought about having to line up like a school girl to have her nails inspected and she a mature, adult person. But I never asked her at the time. In fact we rarely discussed such things — on duty or off.

We might moan among ourselves and grumble over petty inconveniences or when we thought some extra chore was something we shouldn't be doing. But the wider aspects of things — the life we led bound in service to others — well, we never saw anything wrong with it, so we never talked about it. It was a way of life — our way of life. It was all we knew. Life might be better on the other side of the wall, but then none of us had ever been there to see for ourselves. So we stayed put — in a world we knew. We were secure. We were happy. We were sad. At times we liked the job — at other times we hated it because of the monotony. But as far as I knew, other people's jobs were exactly the same — sometimes good, sometimes bad. Other folk had boring and happy times all rolled into one life. So had I. My idea was to do the job well — to work hard and do things as best I could. I wanted praise. I resented being told off — well, not resented it; it's truer to say I was disappointed whenever the cook found fault with my work. But when I stood there every morning in the kitchen after nearly three hours of hard work cleaning things and preparing the staff breakfast, I never once felt any real animosity about having the cook look me up and down to see if my uniform was clean. She had her job to do. I had mine. Anyway, I suppose I was dreaming of the day when I would be a cook like her and it would be me doing the inspecting and dishing-out the praise or the criticism. I expect this dream of mine prevented me from feeling any real resentment.

So, before breakfast every morning the cook would give us all the once-over to see we were presentable to the rest of the staff. She had no intention of letting the side down — of appearing in the dining hall in front of the other servants with the members of her own department not up to scratch. There was usually a deep rivalry between the kitchen and household staffs; not so much between the kitchen maids and the housemaids, but between housekeeper, butler and cook. More often than not it was just a professional affair, each one thinking that his or her own department was a cut above the others and more important in the scale of things within the house. They would act very formally and be completely aloof when talking to each other in front of the staff, but get them on their own and they'd be laughing and joking — completely friendly.

In our case, however, the cook and the butler did not see eye to eye. And their dislike of each other was no pretence. It was for real. Along the passage we would go to the breakfast table in time to be seated at eight o'clock and there in the hall would be gathered the rest of the staff — the head housemaid and three maids, the footman and the butler, the lady's-maid and the two laundry maids. We always entered the room as close to eight o'clock as possible so that everybody else would already be there. It was a sort of grand entrance. The cook liked it this way. You could see it in her face. She never varied the habit the whole time I was there. The butler sat at one end of the table and the cook sat at the other. It was obvious they wanted to be as far away from each other as possible. Whenever their eyes would meet they'd look daggers at each other which, as you can imagine, was not the most pleasant of atmospheres in which to eat a meal — especially the first meal of the day.

As a general rule there really was quite often a great deal of jealousy between butlers and cooks in country houses. The cook always felt that the butler might be on better terms with the laird and his wife than she was — and vice versa. And neither could bear it if they thought the other was getting favoured and they were losing out on something. It was a common occurrence — you expected to find this wee bit of friction, of hostility, between the butler and the cook wherever you might go to work. And on occasions it wasn't just a little bit of friction, but total all-out war.

When you think of it, it was stupid really because living in a close-knit community as we did, all under the same roof, sharing the same table, it was extremely important that everyone should get along well with each other. Such constant bickering sometimes put us all on edge, but in our case the cook and the butler took good care to do their quarrelling out of earshot of her ladyship or the laird. It was absolute nonsense for either of them to think the gentry thought more of one than the other. The butler was good at his job. So, too, was the cook. They'd no need to think of each other as rivals. Basically speaking, the lady of the house treated them in like fashion — with restrained courtesy. As for the laird — well, he talked to each of them in the same way, just as he did to all of us; with a bit of a joke; easily, not stuffy or aloof at all. He talked plainly. He had great charm. And yet, if the butler saw the cook having a conversation with either the laird or his wife he'd be needling at the cook for ages trying to discover what had been said. And she was just as bad. What a pair.

Lord, it's not as if the pair of them had nothing to do. Their day was just as busy as ours, in its own fashion. I suppose it was just another case of human nature at work. No doubt they disliked each other at first sight. So, out of pettiness and spite, each decided to make a misery of the other's life. And they succeeded. Oh yes, they certainly achieved their aim. And in a strange way it never seemed to make either of them down-hearted or dispirited in any way. They seemed to enjoy it. To thrive on it. The pair of them. The trouble was, all of us maids were caught in the cross-fire. And we didn't like it — not one tiny bit.

The staff ate all their meals together; breakfast at 8a.m., lunch at 11.45a.m., and the evening meal, a sort of high tea, at 6p.m. Our meals were different from those served upstairs, but if there had been anything left over from the previous day, part of a roast, a pie, this sort of thing, it came to the servants' table. But usually we were on stews and things, rabbits done in all sorts of different ways or hare — common stuff, I suppose some folks might think, but there was always plenty of it — and it was good. A darned sight better than the food many ordinary people were eating at the time. We got quite a lot of meat, really, which was something a great number of ordinary working people in the 1920s found difficult to get hold of because, quite simply, they hadn't the money to buy it. We were lucky in this respect. We were never in danger of starving. There was always a stock pot on the range — for soups and stews, things of this kind. So we were all well catered for.

Mind you, with our last meal being at six o'clock in the evening we were sometimes pretty hungry by the time the gentry had finished their dinner and we had seen to all the washing and tidying-up and stacking of the plates. So we had a cup of tea or cocoa or even coffee, sometimes, with a sandwich or a biscuit — this would be around 10.30p.m. But very often if there was a great deal to do it might be 11.30 or nearly midnight before we could put our feet up. Then, with the cocoa drunk and the sandwich eaten, it was time to get off to bed. And it's no exaggeration to say that we couldn't wait to get to bed. As soon as my head used to touch the pillow I'd be off to sleep. I never had any sleepless nights. They were never a part of my life. I was usually too tired. Dead-beat. And no wonder — having to rise every morning at 4.45.

Still, us underlings weren't the only ones up and about to all hours of the night. The cook's hours of work were just the same when it came to the evenings. She was always there, right up to the last, to see that everything was completed satisfactorily and all plates, pots and pans put away in a tidy fashion. And the butler, he was upstairs making sure that his silver was all stored away, properly cleaned and shining brightly. Oh yes, they were there too. So, to be fair, although I, and others like me, had to slave on all day, our superiors were every bit as tied to their jobs as we were. It was long hours for everybody. We may have been their inferiors, well down the scale of things in the jobs hierarchy, but at least in this respect we were their equals.

There was a holiday rota prepared for everyone on the staff. We all had two weeks off every year. Early in the year you had your first week and then towards the end of the year came the second week. We got paid for our holidays, which was quite something because I knew of some estates where, when you went on holiday, they just docked your wages for the time you were off. I expect it was one way of ensuring that their staff never took holidays — that they were always there, able to work. But gradually this sort of Victorian behaviour towards employees died out, even on estates, places that usually resist change right up to the last possible moment, and it became the general custom throughout the country to grant holidays with pay. A few die-hards lingered on, mind you, among the lairds, but fairly soon they, too, were forced into doing as others did. They had to change their tune. Circumstances were against them. They found that employees were leaving them and going off to work on more enlightened estates where they could receive decent treatment.

Our holiday rota had its drawbacks, all the same. My holiday always seemed to land on the third week of the month. As we were only paid right at the end of the month this meant I never had any money to spend while on holiday, except perhaps for a few shillings scrimped and saved from my meagre wage of 13s.6d. a week. Luckily, this didn't bother me too much, because very few people of our kind ever would go anywhere on holiday at that time. Oh yes, perhaps a day out in the nearest town or a day on the coast somewhere, if you could reach the seaside easily by bus or train. But there were no weeks in far-off places, package holidays to sunny Spain and Majorca, such as the bulk of people go in for nowadays. No, we just went home to spend our free time with our parents and brothers and sisters. I was fortunate in that I only lived six miles or so away from the estate. I was usually driven home by the chauffeur who would be making the journey to town in any case. And at the end of the week he'd call in and take me back to the Big House again.

Like most good things in short supply, holidays in those days were greatly appreciated. No matter how much you might enjoy the job it was certainly a relief to get away for a week from the confined atmosphere of the house — the claustrophobia of estate life. A week in your own home seemed to put things right so that when you went back to work you did so, to some extent, looking forward to seeing the old place again; yes, even in a strange way not caring about having to get up so early in the mornings and work such long hours. It was our world, the only one we knew and when holidays came round the prospect of doing something different for a week was really welcomed because of the chance it gave us to get away to a change of scenery and fresh company. Nowadays, good long holidays are a part of everyone's job — or they should be — and this is a wonderful thing. It makes people realize that there's more to life than work, slaving away throughout the year on behalf of others as we all had to do. It's good that the worker has the chance of doing something for himself or herself now — and the free time to really enjoy life. I had plenty of enjoyment during my early working years, despite the drudgery imposed by the routine in a country house kitchen. But freedom — that's one thing I never had. While I was a kitchen maid that's something I knew nothing about.

CHAPTER
NINE

Although there might have been little freedom in the daily working life of someone employed in the Strathalder kitchen, at least, in the main, there was not much contact, other than by the cook, with either the laird or his wife. The work of a kitchen maid was not subject to their daily scrutiny. For the members of the household staff it was an entirely different matter. If a housemaid failed to dust properly or was unsuccessful in putting a polish on the furniture, her lapses were quite likely to be detected by the lady of the house who would, without hesitation, issue any reprimand herself. Because they were always in close proximity to the laird, his wife, family and any guests who happened to be staying in the mansion house, an especially rigid code of conduct was expected from members of the household staff, an attitude that even extended, as far as the women were concerned, to how they behaved themselves in their off-duty time.

Grace Macarthur, one of the housemaids, remembers that above all else the restrictions imposed on her colleagues and herself were among the most common causes of grievance when she was in service in the early 1930s.

One of my main grumbles, especially when I was in my early days in service, in my late teens and early twenties, was the ridiculously early hour I was expected to be back at the Big House if I had an evening off, even a day off for that matter. There were three of us — myself at nineteen and two other girls, twenty-two and twenty-eight, I think. Our time off was worked like this; we each had a day off every week and one Sunday a month. And, unless you asked special permission to be late we had to be in by 9p.m., if we were away from the House. It didn't matter what age you were — it was just the same for me, the youngest, as it was for the eldest. We were all treated alike. Of course, if I was going to a dance, and whenever there was one in the locality I tried to arrange things so that I could be off work and free to go, this permission was usually given for me to stay out late, normally until 11p.m., but sometimes to 11.30 if her ladyship was in a generous mood.

One reason for this rule, apart from the usual idea common among the gentry at that time that servants, especially the women, had to be kept on a tight rein in case of scandal (utterly ridiculous, of course), was that in this household there were prayers almost every evening, usually at 9.30. The prayers took place when there was no late dinner being served — that was the only occasion when religion was scrapped. After the ladies came out of the drawing room and the men from the dining room they mustered in the main hall of the house, where we servants joined them. A section of the Bible would be read and the laird said the prayer for the day. It followed the same pattern every night — Bible reading, the prayer and then everyone joining in to sing "The Lord's My

Shepherd". After that you got off to your bed or, if there was still work to be done, you just went back and carried on.

You didn't dress up to go to prayers. If you were working (in my case I might be doing my evening chores, seeing to the bedroom fires, filling hot water bottles and putting them into the beds) you left whatever you were doing and went down to prayers. When they were over you got on with the job straightaway again. No time for slacking. I suppose the laird thought this ritual with the prayers, his prayer meeting as he called it, was good for our souls. Oh, I know he meant well. He was, after all, a kind enough individual. But it always struck me as strange that for ten minutes, or maybe fifteen minutes or so, here we all were, servants and master, gathered in the same room, singing the same psalm. And yet, he had everything in life he could have wished for — and we had nothing. Or at best precious little. In a way the religion was making us equal even although it was only for a few minutes in each day. Despite the fact we were into the 1930s the gentry were still clinging to the old ways. They were still reluctant to let go although ever since the end of the First World War and right throughout the 1920s a new outlook was developing among the people who worked for them. But, as yet, they weren't prepared to accept that changes were afoot, that they were bound to overtake them sooner or later. In a way for them to recognize that change was around the corner would have been admitting defeat. Most of them didn't want to know. They wanted to go on living in style as they had done for many years and their ancestors before them. To allow for changes in the general working conditions of the likes of us would have meant them lowering their standard of living. It didn't matter a hoot to most of them that our standards needed to be raised. For the majority of the gentry their opposition took the form of simply carrying on with their traditional way of life. I think they hoped that if they took no notice then all this talk of change might simply go away. And they could be left in peace — as before.

More and more of us younger ones in domestic service were beginning to question some of the petty rules and restrictions placed upon us — the long hours we had to work and the general attitude of many employers that we were in some way inferior (very inferior) beings. Not that this was the attitude on this estate. The laird and his wife and family were, basically speaking, quite decent people. But there were many of their kind with estates who thought people like us were mere peasants. All the same, when I'm speaking about the decent behaviour by the laird and his wife towards us, I am, in a way, being too kind, too generous, to her ladyship. She was very much a law unto herself and although she made a great show of trying to make it appear she was genuinely interested in the welfare of her staff, it was really more a case of her being (you'll excuse the language) a bloody nosey-parker. She was always poking about, enquiring about this or that and while some used to say, "My isn't it good of her to take so much trouble", it wasn't long before I saw through her methods. It became quite obvious to me that she wasn't really interested in us. It was all a show.

Let me give you one instance. The cook, a woman in her late twenties, early thirties, became ill. Yes, she was young to be holding down such a responsible job, but she was a first-rate cook. Really excellent at every aspect of her job. She was confined to her bed and after a couple of days when there was no sign of her condition improving, in fact she appeared to be getting worse, one of the estate workers' wives who was a good cook was brought in to take over her job until she got better. At the same time her ladyship sent for the local doctor, but by the time he managed to pay a visit later that day, a baby — a wee boy — was born to the cook. Then there was fun and games. Oh my, not only were we surprised — she was a big, hefty woman and none of us had any idea of her being pregnant, in fact it's the last thing we would have thought of being the matter with her — but her ladyship — well, she almost went off her head with rage and bad temper. She was so wild, so bitter, because just like the staff she, too, had failed to notice the cook's condition, that our lives were made a misery for days as she flung one tantrum after another. She found fault with everything; in my case dust where I'd never expected her to look, some brasswork around a fireplace not properly cleaned. Not only was she morally shocked that an unmarried woman should give birth under her roof, but she was angry because the woman was such a splendid cook and, good cooks being thin on the ground, she knew it would be difficult to find a replacement of the same quality.

So, once the cook was able to get up from her bed she was dismissed and sent packing, baby and all. She wasn't denied a reference, but it was a poor un-Christian thing to do to her. If her ladyship hadn't been such an uncharitable soul and had practised religion in the way she tried to impose it on us then she would have retained the poor woman as her cook. She could quite easily have let her have her old job back and attached the baby onto the household by arranging to pay for it to be looked after by one of the woman's relations, or even by one of the estate wives. I've heard of this being done on several occasions when, due to some circumstance or other, a good servant found herself in a similar plight. Whatever, if she had been a proper lady she would have behaved with dignity and compassion, set an example — but oh no, she just went on grumbling about it being a slur on the house and making other daft statements of this kind. Instead of accepting what had happened and showing some decency to the cook who, as you can imagine, was depressed enough as it was by finding herself an unmarried mother, her ladyship railed and ranted at her until I'm positive she was glad to see the back of the place.

I never forgave her ladyship for her callous and stupid behaviour. She was never the same person to me after that. I'd see her flouncing along in the garden or in the house chatting to her fine friends and I'd think to myself, "What right have you got to think of yourself as a lady?" I could never again think of her as being one, not after seeing her in such a temper and hearing her shouting at the top of her voice behind the closed doors of the drawing room, "But why was I never told long before this?" A true lady would have taken things in her stride and been an example to us all. But not her. She was just too selfish, too proud; absolutely lacking in tolerance.

Mind you, some of the older staff didn't see things my way. They were in favour of what her ladyship had done. To them, the cook was a sinner. And what made things worse in their eyes — she appeared to be an unrepentant sinner. But among the young maids, both in the house and the kitchen, and even from the two young footmen, no more than lads, the cook had plenty of sympathy and attention. So, in a way, we gave her what support we could when the one woman who could have changed the course of her life turned her back on her. It was sad, but at least it opened my eyes, made me aware of the nasty side to some people's nature. I started to think more positively about things after that day.

All the same, there were some really happy occasions — bright times when we servants had our bit of fun. One evening the entire household — laird, wife and guests who were staying there for the shooting — went out to dinner on a neighbouring estate. So, once they were off, safely out of sight down the drive, the staff got going and we had a party of our own. We'd known for several days that they'd all be away this particular evening, so the cook and the kitchen maids got busy baking and preparing sandwiches so that when the occasion arrived we would have a nice spread awaiting us. It took place in the servants' hall, which was a huge room. We just pushed the dining table back to the side against a wall and there was plenty of space for us all to move around. Music was provided by the governess on the piano; she was always ready to take part in any fun. There was also a gramophone so we had plenty of music for any dancing and singing.

The two footmen and some of the young gardeners from the bothy were partners for any of us who felt like dancing and even the butler attended although I don't remember him taking to the floor. Well, we were in really good form, the party going with a swing, when someone said they thought they'd heard a car on the drive at the front of the house. It was only about 9.30p.m. and as we weren't expecting anybody back until between 11.30 and midnight no one bothered very much. So, as you can well imagine, I got quite a shock to hear a knock on the door of the servants' hall. I

141

remember quite distinctly I had a huge slice of cake in one hand when I opened the door and I almost dropped it when I saw in the corridor four of the household guests — three men and a young woman. "What's going on?" one of them asked, looking past me into the crowded room where several couples were high-stepping the Lancers to a piano accompaniment. "We're having a party," I managed to stammer, my face red. I thought to myself, "This is it. There'll be a fine hue and cry now when her ladyship gets to hear about this carry-on." The cook came to my rescue and asked if the visitors would like to join in the fun and they accepted readily.

Seemingly, for some reason or other, they'd left their dinner party early, intending to have a good night's sleep before the next day's shooting. But when they joined us they forgot about their good intentions and were with us to the finish. They were good mixers and danced and sang with the rest of us.

They never told her ladyship — or the laird — about our revelry. In fact, the following day one of the men stopped me in a corridor where I was doing some dusting and said that they had all enjoyed themselves. He added that our party had been a much livelier affair than the dinner party to which they had been invited. There was a twinkle in his eyes when he said this and I knew exactly what he meant. I passed the message on around the rest of the staff and for the remainder of their stay in the house we all made sure in quiet, discreet ways that our four "special guests" were given preferential treatment. Our secret was in safe hands.

The drawing room was one of the nicest rooms in the house, furnished in the best of style and on the walls hung paintings and tapestries. And the chairs were mostly all covered with tapestries that former ladies of the house had made. A few had even been made by the laird's wife at that time. Her ladyship was quite an expert with a needle, very good at embroidery; in fact needlework of any kind. Sometimes she'd spend hours every day working at one of her tapestries, especially in the winter months.

I did envy her for that — oh, just for having the free time to sit around and spend it doing exactly as she pleased. I was fairly keen on needlework myself, having been shown the ropes by my mother, but I had few opportunities to indulge myself by practising it as a hobby. There were times when there were no guests in the house and I'd take in her afternoon tea and there she would be, sitting working away beside a log fire, sewing quietly and peacefully, shaping the most elaborate pattern. And I couldn't help thinking how I would like to change places with her. Even for a few hours. It would have been like a dream coming true. I never admitted to her that I, too, liked needlework because I've no doubt I would have ended up darning holes in socks and stockings, mending shirts, this sort of thing which, of course, was not my idea of fun at all.

I think she would have found it hard to appreciate that one of her housemaids was interested in using a needle solely for the object of creating beautiful designs and patterns. It would never have occurred to her that this could be so. To her, needlework of the kind she did, was something for a lady of leisure to do; far too refined and genteel for the likes of me to indulge in. I'm not blaming her for having this attitude, merely recording it as a fact of life as it was in those times. She wasn't alone among those of her class in thinking this way — far from it. So I kept my mouth shut and beyond passing a few admiring remarks, which seemed to please her, I just went on working normally and dreamed of the day when I could sit at my own fireside, be waited on hand and foot and sew all day long, doing just as I pleased — when I pleased. Some dream.

I daren't think of the number of hours I spent in that drawing room dusting and polishing the furniture. There was a collection of small tables, all of which had to be polished until you could see your reflection in their surface. The smell of the wax we used has stayed with me to this day; a sweet, heavy scent like one of those old-fashioned roses. This used to fill the room by the time I'd finished and despite the hard work it was really something to smell that and see everything shining — and know you had done a good job of work. Least, you thought you had done a good job, perhaps, until either her ladyship or the housekeeper found something out of place or dust in a place where you were expected to have been. But I always enjoyed working in that room because, really, it was such a beautiful place to be; the tables with their ornaments — valuable antiques, I'm sure — the paintings, the tapestries and the alcoves always filled with flowers, great blooms and displays of the very best from the gardens. At times they were changed every day, so there was always plenty of variety; roses, chrysanthemums, dahlias — oh, and dozens of other kinds I couldn't name then and still can't put a name to now. The room had two enormous bay windows facing a lawn and on the opposite side above the river was a steep bank covered with trees of all kinds. It was a splendid outlook.

I took an extra pride in my work when I was in that room. It seemed right when everything was so perfect that I should give of my very best in order to keep it that way. I took pride in my work, not just because it was expected of me, but because I wanted to make sure that everything was kept in good order. A great deal of care and hard work had gone into the making of some of the furniture — you could see the craftsmanship in every table and chair — and it was only right that with my duster and polish I, too, should play my part in preserving them, showing them off to best advantage. There's no more splendid sight than a table, say in rosewood or mahogany, with its top shining and sparkling. Sometimes I go on outings and visit country houses and castles — stately homes they call them — and the first thing I do when I enter a drawing room or dining room is to look at the tables. If there's a good shine on them I know they're being well cared for. And if that's the case then there's a good chance the whole house is not just a museum of the past, but that a real attempt is being made to show it to the visitors as it must have appeared at one time to those people who lived in the rooms.

These new woods and surfaces they're putting on tables nowadays may look shiny, but it's all just a surface gloss. On the old tables, the ones I once polished, the shine was deep, so thick you could almost feel you could cut it with a knife. And it got there by sweat and hard work, rubbing this way and that, first one cloth, then another, rubbing and rubbing until your wrists and elbows ached and there before your eyes appeared the gloss — the result of all your hard labour. I think I could call myself an expert on polishing. That's no idle boast. I should know all about it. If I had a pound note for every table and sideboard I've polished in my lifetime then I would be a very rich woman today.

All the same, I may not be well-off, but I'm happy. I was happy then, as a housemaid, despite all the silly problems and difficulties. I'm happy now — now that I'm able to sit back and remember. And in this world if you're happy with your lot, then that counts for a great deal. Don't you agree?

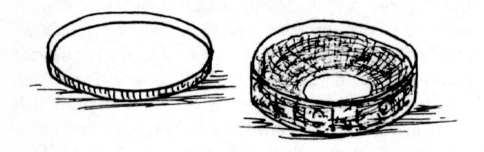

CHAPTER
TEN

The laird's children in modern times are, like their contemporaries, educated in much the same fashion as everyone else. They go to school, then college, perhaps even to university. Few will attend the local State schools. Even in today's more open, ostensibly classless, society the breath of change that has passed across the mouldering traditions of Scottish country estate life has not been sufficiently powerful to extend as far as this. In this one respect, at least, there is still a tendency to cling to the established method of education for the children of the landed class — to send them to public schools. They go to a preparatory school, then on to one of the many boarding schools of varying size and standards. In one respect there is nothing remarkable in such a situation. The lairds are not alone. Thousands of middle-class parents in Britain do exactly the same thing — for better or worse.

Life for the children of the laird begins in the care of a nanny, someone to take over from the mother the responsibilities of every aspect of their early upbringing. The role of the nanny is well documented in English literature; once a figure to be found in every Victorian and Edwardian upper-and middle-class

home, her role in society is now, almost exclusively, confined to the world of the laird in his country home or the wealthy businessman whose style of life is modelled on that of the laird. But while nannies were concerned solely with the day-to-day rearing of the children placed in their care, it was to a governess that the laird and his wife turned when the child was old enough to start absorbing some element of education.

The position of the governess at Strathalder is, like on every estate, something from the past history of the place. They came and went, instructing the children in a variety of everyday subjects, reading, writing, history, geography, until at the age of twelve or thirteen it was time for more formal teaching in an organized school. Governesses went on educating their young charges throughout the estates of Scotland until at least the start of the Second World War. Until then it was an accepted means of imparting education. Now, schools of various sorts attend to this no matter how privileged the background of the child.

Dorothy Saunders recalls that the governess was sometimes a lonely person amid the teeming staff of a country mansion house. Because she was in daily contact with the children and, as a result, in close proximity to the laird and his wife, other members of the household staff were often unable to decide whose side the governess was on. Her own personal background was usually quite different to that of most of the women on the staff and this, too, was instrumental in ensuring that she was set apart from everyone else.

There were times when you felt — how can I best describe it? — a very separate person; not quite on a level with your employer and at some distance from the rest of the staff. The very nature of your job saw to this because a major part of every day was spent in the company of the laird's children and, quite often, in conversation with his wife. Of course if one was sensible one appreciated right at the start that such a situation was likely to develop. I always took great care to see that I never became depressed or in any way worried by it.

Some governesses were distinctly aloof people, not only from the others on the staff, but from the gentry as well. It was as if they thought of themselves as a special race of chosen people; a race apart, a separate class if you like to think of it in this way. They were solely concerned with their own lives and those of the children in their care. Anyone else was of no consequence whatsoever. It was remarkably easy to start thinking in this way. As a governess you were responsible only to the lady of the house and so, in a way, you became marked as a distinctive individual. All the same, much depended on her ladyship herself as to how the governess behaved.

You see, some of the wives of the gentry seemed to take little interest in their children. Well, this is how it appeared to me and I had several posts in my time, all with employers of vastly different natures. You got the type who was quite content to leave the education and the welfare of the children in your hands and who would never interfere with your decisions; yet, at the same time, they managed to form a good relationship with their own children. And there were others who treated the children with indifference, yet at the slightest chance would be dictating and laying down the law and making my job more difficult because their sudden interest was usually, more often than not, merely a passing whim; and having created a fuss and caused confusion not only in the minds of the children but with myself, they'd forget just as quickly and go back to their former, indifferent behaviour until the next opportunity arose. One never knew exactly how one stood with people like that. Of course, the children must have felt the same way as I did; thoroughly confused.

My general attitude was to take the view that I had been employed to give the children a good and widely-based education. I was the expert. And, as such, should be left to get on with the job I was being paid to do. This approach invariably worked — to everyone's satisfaction. It may sound arrogant, but I can assure you it wasn't. Any sensible employer was able to understand perfectly well — and accepted the situation. I never had any excuse for them if they didn't. I always made the point quite clear at the initial interview.

Unlike some governesses I have known, who looked with disdain or, perhaps more accurately to use a word I expressed earlier, with indifference, on the other members of the staff, I always tried to become absorbed into the life of the staff side of the household. It was hard, mind you, because having a special position I was sometimes regarded with some suspicion due to my having such close contact with the lady of the house. I also had my own separate quarters, sitting room, bedroom and bathroom alongside the children's wing of the house. But the more sensible among the staff soon began to appreciate that in no way was I a sort of spy in their midst and before too long my attempts at being friendly and

151

always willing to join in the fun whenever there was any were welcomed quite naturally and I was accepted.

The governess did not eat with the rest of the staff. She always dined in the nursery with her charges. So this tended to cut one off in quite a formidable manner from the other staff members. This dining with the children went on until they might be ten or eleven — considered old enough to take their place among adults in the dining room.

I was answerable directly to the lady of the house and, at the onset of my time in charge of the children, a programme of work was agreed upon. Naturally, it was the prerogative of the parents to tell me which subjects I had to teach. But I always tried to make it clear that much would depend on the ability of the individual child to absorb and master the chosen curriculum. It was very much a case of trial and error in the early stages, because one had to develop a rapport with one's charges and tread a fine line between appearing to be too much of a disciplinarian and someone whom the children could take advantage of at every available opportunity. Of course, one had to allow a certain amount of latitude with their behaviour. All young children learn better if they feel they are not too hemmed-in by restrictions and rules. But while giving them this freedom it was always important to impress on them quite firmly at the very beginning of our time together, that in all matters within the nursery and schoolroom I was in charge. My word was the law.

It was harder to achieve this when the parents were either of the kind who had no idea of the ways of young children or who, quite simply, thought their offspring could do no wrong. It might surprise you to know just how many were in the latter category. And children, being children, were quick to realize that such a situation existed. They then began to use it to their own advantage, telling tales behind one's back; in fact, doing all they could to make life as awkward and as difficult as possible.

Sometimes the reason for this state of affairs was that they had been in the charge of a weak nanny before I arrived on the scene. The normal pattern was that the children would be in the care of a nanny from birth until the age of five. At this stage I would take over and all being well I would stay with them until they were ready to go to school at the age of twelve or, perhaps, if they were slow learners, thirteen. Quite often I would arrive to find myself confronted by a spoiled, sulky child — or even worse, a pair of them. And then, of course, one's initial months were not so much taken up with teaching them anything, but in trying to rid them of this selfish trait in their character. Sometimes, I succeeded. Most times, actually. There were a few failures. You can see them around today — arrogant and self-opinionated, which characteristics, when they were youngsters, they displayed to the full and I could do nothing to change. It seemed inherent; very often their parents were exactly the same.

But don't get me wrong. I would not wish to create the impression that the estate proprietors' children were any worse — or indeed, any better — than others around them in various classes of life. Indeed, on the whole, they were no different. All had good points and bad points. Some were charming — indeed the majority of the ones with whom I came into contact were like this; a delight to teach and to be with and who, today, in adulthood, still keep in regular touch with me.

I taught them every conceivable thing; reading, writing, simple mathematics, history, geography, and a range of arts and crafts — piano playing, violin playing, harp playing, sewing and knitting.

A room in the nursery wing was set aside as a schoolroom and fitted-out as such with individual desks and a blackboard. In fact it resembled a schoolroom in every way except for the number of pupils; most likely there would be two, sometimes three or four.

I think I managed to do a reasonable job with most of my charges. There's no doubt that given a child with a lively, enquiring mind then he or she benefited greatly from individual tuition given by a governess; more so than could possibly be managed at one of the preparatory schools now used for their counterparts today. One had the opportunity to develop skills and talents at an extremely early age, much the best time to do it. If a child showed an aptitude for playing a particular musical instrument it was possible to allow this interest to develop, to bring it to maturity. The same thing applied to poetry and literature. It was so much easier to impart one's own enthusiasms, one's likes and dislikes in the field of literature to, say, a couple of children in this special atmosphere than it would have been to a class full of children of differing intelligence and interest.

Yes, in a way it was a privileged society. There is no point in denying this. For my part I think I was always aware of this fact. Indeed, I'm sure I was. I know I felt I was privileged to share such a household with those who owned it. I came from a fairly ordinary city family — middle-class is what we would be called nowadays — and not only was I intrigued by the life-style of such people as the lairds and their families, but I had been fascinated by country life ever since I'd first been taken as a little girl, by my parents for a holiday in a small village in the Scottish Highlands.

I taught my charges as best I could — to the best of my ability. I could do no more than that. This is how I expressed myself to the very few parents who found fault with my methods of tuition. I can only do my best, is how I used to put it. Nine times out of ten, they were satisfied. The tenth? — well, that was usually the sort of person who would never be satisfied with a single thing unless they did it themselves. And very often this is what used to happen. There was a particularly strong grape-vine of information about employers running between all the various governesses. The same went for nannies. We knew who were the good employers and who were the bad; who were the ones who left the governess alone to get on with her job and who were continually interfering and causing problems. And when a governess left the employment of one of the latter kind following a dispute, word of the truth of the situation, the real circumstances surrounding it, was soon passed around.

The sensible governess in the know would stay clear of applying for a post in such a household. Of course, they always found someone to fill the post — eventually. And when we heard of this we'd wait to see how long it would be before the new incumbent resigned — or was dismissed. One household I knew of had nine governesses in as many years. And yet they could never see, never appreciate, that it was they who were in the wrong; that it was their attitude, or in this case, the attitude of the lady of the house, that was driving the governesses away. Good, capable people were forced to seek posts elsewhere because they refused to be treated as if their knowledge and professional opinions were of no consequence.

I like to think that I imparted quite a considerable amount of knowledge to the children entrusted to me. Perhaps this sounds stuffy, even pompous. It's not meant to be, I can assure you of that. I just believe I was able to give those children some insight into the life that lay beyond the boundaries of their parents' estate. Certainly I like to think that today when some of them pick up a good book or hear and enjoy a fine piece of music they are doing so because I sowed the first seed of interest in their minds all those years ago.

It was always a sad day for me when they reached the age of twelve or thirteen and boarding schools had been found for them — and they were ready for off. It was especially sad if I had enjoyed living in the household for seven or eight years or so and there was no younger child to enable me to continue. And away they would go, often with tearful faces, probably the first time they had ever been isolated from the protection of their parents; and I'd wave to them, then pack my bags and make my own departure — more dignified, perhaps, but just as sad, just as heart-wrenching. And melancholy thoughts would stay with me, memories of the happy times I'd had, until I was firmly established in the new household, beginning the process all over again.

The amusing thing is that on more than one occasion I overheard one lady saying to another, "I really don't know why we bother to send the children to school. They learn just as much at home with a governess. As far as I can gather they seem to have too easy a time and do next to nothing, just play among themselves when they're away."

156

I would smile and, of course, say nothing. But it was pleasing to know that one's capabilities were rated more highly than some of the most expensive boarding schools, the most eagerly sought after, in the land. No one could have asked for a higher testimonial, a better tribute to one's profession. Because, you see, in many cases that lady's opinion was perfectly right. Absolutely correct.

CHAPTER
ELEVEN

The gardens at Strathalder are surrounded by high stone walls, the mortar pockmarked and chipped, in places green with the moss that clings to the surface after more than a century exposed to the rain and mist sweeping down from mountain peaks visible beyond the trees. There are two gardens; the one closest to the mansion house, a mass of herbaceous plants crowding and spilling over from the wide borders flanking the paths and clusters of shrubs arranged in groups so that height and the colour of the flowers are immediately visible from any corner of the expanse. The second garden is reached through a wrought-iron gate set into one wall, the old kitchen garden which covers several acres. Much of it is now derelict and unkempt, one corner a wilderness of grass and sprawling gooseberry bushes, another just like it left to revert to nature where, in summer, butterflies swamp the rampant buddleia bushes with their sprays of white and crimson and deep mauve flowers. On the south-facing wall espalier fruit trees, apple, pear and plum, once pruned and trained to grow as required along the wires provided for their framework of branches, now run wild, their gnarled and knotted limbs grey and silver,

green and yellow from the profusion of lichens and mosses flourishing unhindered amid a world of neglect.

From 1918 until the mid-1930s as many as fourteen gardeners worked within the confines of the walls; at any one time there were never fewer than ten. Now, there is only one gardener who, when he requires additional help, employs on a part-time basis a retired gardener who lives in the nearby village.

Like the gardens of all mansion houses in the countryside, the Strathalder gardens were, in their prime, a place of abundance; where flowers were grown for decoration and display in the house and vegetables of all kinds for use in the kitchen. Today, flowers and vegetables still follow the same route, but there are fewer of them. The large greenhouses are two-thirds full of tomatoes for sale to local shops and any other surplus produce is also sold off in an attempt to defray the general cost of maintenance. A few estate gardens in the area are now fully commercial enterprises — market gardens in more distinguished settings than most. But Strathalder remains unchanged by the pressures of the commercial world; although only a shadow remains of the gardens' grandeur in former years, they are still, primarily, enjoyed for their peace and privacy.

Gone, however, are the trim boxwood borders which once fringed every bed within the gardens and where at one time the paths were hoed by an army of men and boys, lifting the weeds clear of the soil and the gravel; chemical weedkillers are now sprayed upon the ground by one man with the apparatus strapped to his back.

The entire job is completed annually within a couple of days when once it would have been a source of occupation for much of the year. The paths threading across the lawn from the house to the river and those that run along the banks beside the water are treated in the same fashion; the minimum amount of work being done in order to keep them open unlike in the past, when their care and attention was the pride and joy of many an estate worker. A mower towed by a tractor from the Home Farm now cuts the great swathes of lawn; all appears tidy and organized, neat and efficient. In one respect, on the surface, it undoubtedly is; but this minimal attention devoted to the maintenance of appearances can never, in any way, hope to match the boundless care once lavished on gardens and grounds when labour was plentiful — and cheap.

Bob Williamson became a gardener at such a time; at the end of the First World War. But when he looks back on the changes he has witnessed in the structure of estate life, it is not so much the day-to-day work in the gardens that he remembers; it is the feeling, the intense secure experience, of being part of a real community, guided and directed by the laird. It is something which most older people mention and recall with some degree of pride.

In the 1920s, indeed before this time, during the First World War and further back, there was a good deal of class division in Britain; feelings which brought bitterness, yes, and sometimes outright hatred between the working classes and those who had money and riches. But up here on the estate we saw little, if any, of such differences of opinion. The whole atmosphere on this estate and probably on most similar places was one of harmony; it was like being a member of one big family. The laird and his wife looked on all their employees, yes, and their tenants too, the farmers who paid rent to them — everybody, workers and tenants — as being individuals under their care and protection. If they heard of any illness or trouble where they could possibly be of some assistance they were very good at going to pay a visit. There was always what I felt to be a genuine interest on their part in everybody connected with the estate. Maybe her ladyship wasn't what you might have described as the first-class lady in other respects, but even with her this interest was there.

Between Christmas and the New Year there were three nights set aside by the laird for entertaining the farmers, the tenants in the houses and the staff. The farmers and their wives were usually invited to the first night, then the tenants and their wives and the staff. On the final night it was the turn of the children. They got everything that was left.

All the parties took place in the main hall of the mansion house. Buffet meals were prepared by the cook, the kitchen maid and the scullery maid and the butler and the footmen, they looked after all the setting-out of it to make it as attractive as possible. Chairs covered with tartan rugs and cloth were placed all around the walls of the hall and in the lamp light, with all the decorations, bunches of holly covered in red berries and sprays and clusters of other greenery hanging from the ceiling, pinned above the doors and windows, the place looked splendid.

The laird and his wife — and the family when they were old enough — attended every night and every person who was a guest at each party received a gift when they left. If it was a farmer's wife she usually got a cake, a square cake, and if the man smoked it would likely be tobacco and matches. If he didn't smoke then more often than not the gift would be a half bottle of whisky. There were few men who didn't drink. They all got something and although the gifts were usually the same for everybody — cakes for the women, tobacco or whisky for the men, they were accepted quite freely in the spirit in which they were given. It was a kindly gesture on the part of the laird and his wife and the people on the estate appreciated this act by them both.

No, I don't think the laird simply held those parties because he felt he had to do it. I'm certain he did not think of it as being part of his duty. Certainly there could have been few estates where they didn't take place. I'm sure, in fact I'm absolutely certain, that there was more to it than the gentry just doing what they thought was expected of them. The good ones — like our laird — had no airs or graces about them. Our laird had inherited the place from his father. And so on. There was a tradition, a line of inheritance, running through the family. They were an integral part of the community, one of the foundations of the district. If it hadn't been for their family there would have been no estate — no village close by. Not only had they inherited the estate, but along with it had come the stewardship of the welfare of the people living on the estate. This is what I mean about the family aspect of things. Even as a child you felt you mattered when you were being raised on an estate such as this one.

All the same I found as a gardener that you were still likely to come across folk who, although they were born and brought up in the countryside, seemed to have no idea about how plants grew or the time it took to bring certain flowers and vegetables into season, making them ready for cutting and use.

I was in a place for a time where it was my job to go up to the house every morning for the daily order for vegetables. In this case it was the lady of the house — not the cook — who attended to deciding what was required. This was most unusual, but then her ladyship was a most unusual woman in every respect. Anyway, I'd been planting-out some celery the day before and while I was doing this job her ladyship came past, out for one of her walks. She loved to be always poking about the place, interfering in this and that, generally speaking, wherever she went, making a proper nuisance of herself. She stopped and asked me what I was doing. I told her. "Planting the celery, my lady." Apparently satisfied with this reply she went on her way and I thought no more about it. Well, up I goes to the house the next day for her list of vegetables and there was only one thing she wanted that day. Would you believe it? Celery. And it just newly planted-out. How could you beat that for ignorance? Eh? What an idiot of a woman she was. It took me about five minutes to make her see that it would need a month or two to grow before it was ready for the table. I don't think she believed me. I'm sure she thought I was just being awkward. You see, she was the type who thought she just had to open her mouth and say what she liked and everybody would be doing her bidding. It didn't matter whether or not it was possible. Anyhow, I think she had to make do with carrots that day, instead of the celery. I'm not sure. Whatever it was, she had to wait for her celery. And it didn't please her. No, she was riled for days after that.

164

One place I was at was a huge estate where a pony and cart were used to convey the vegetables from the gardens to the kitchen in the Big House. We had huge loads to carry, with one enormous one every Saturday. That's when I first tasted tomatoes — sitting on the cart on the way up to the Big House.

The foreman who was in charge of the greenhouses was with me at the time. We'd been away to a dance the night before and had drunk too much whisky for our own good. We were both feeling pretty rotten, sore heads, nasty mouths. My mate says, "Try one of these things, man. What a fine taste it will put into your mouth." He handed me a tomato from a pile of them in the cart. I'd seen them growing in the greenhouses, but up to then I'd been working outdoors and had never thought to ask what they might be. Well, I ate it. And by God I enjoyed it. I couldn't get enough of them after that. It was a stroke of luck for me that the stable for my pony was right beside the main greenhouse. I used to nip in and help myself to the tomatoes whenever I could. The foreman used to laugh at my antics and say, "You rogue. That's the worst thing I ever taught you to do — eat tomatoes. I'll have to lock that door when you're about."

But he never did. And I always had plenty of tomatoes.

David Macdonald was born into estate life in the mid-1920s. His father was a gardener, one of twelve employed at the time. Now his son is the only gardener and although he values the traditions of the past as they concern the estate, he has no doubts that modern conditions are preferable to those encountered by his father and others of his generation.

As a youngster you'd be playing around the policies, the grounds, somewhere and the laird would go past in his car. He would wave. You'd wave back. There was something quite friendly and natural about it. And when he went to call on one of his workers — he was often round at my father's house — although, naturally, out of respect for his position he'd be addressed as "sir", he always took pains to be just as formal and correct in speaking to the worker and his wife. He'd call the man by his surname and the wife as "Mrs" so and so. But in the middle of all this formality there was, quite simply, never a moment when he tried to impose his own will, his own superiority. I mean, he had the wealth, the land, the power over you in that he gave you a job. He could just as easily take that job away from you. Without it you'd have been forced to uproot yourself and go miles away from the area you'd probably been born and brought up in. So in this sense alone the laird wielded a fair amount of power. He had the whiphand. But few men who worked for him ever went in fear of him misusing that power. I know it was a terrifying situation for anyone working for a laird who was no gentleman, but then this happened in other walks of life at that time — in the mines and the factories where, in order to keep your job and maybe the roof over your head as well, you had to creep and crawl and generally behave in a subservient fashion. That must have been a degrading experience and there's no doubt about it that abuses of this kind were responsible for the working people in this country hardening their attitude towards the rich. It made them bitter — and hostile.

But it was a mistake then, just as much as it is a mistake today, to believe that just because a person may be wealthy and have an estate (or maybe as far as today is concerned, appear wealthy and own an estate) that he is necessarily intent on treading on the poorer folk, doing down those who work for him. Nowadays you may have mean lairds, real misers who'll hold on to every penny they can and who grumble over quite reasonable expenditure to keep the estate in good order; but I'm fairly certain you'll be hard put to find a tyrant among their number. Types of that nature simply don't exist any more. They have to pay decent wages in order to compete as far as possible with all the industrial places that are now all over this area. Up here, in the north of Scotland, the main drawback to attracting labour to estates is a fairly new phenomenon — the North Sea oil industry. For the first time in their lives men have the opportunity of staying in the area and earning really big money, either at one of the refineries or installations on shore, or in the numerous works that have sprung up all over the place in order to service the industry; they can even find jobs on the rigs themselves out there at sea. Now, this is new and the money so high in most cases that, to be fair, no laird could compete when it comes to wages; in just the same way that local businesses and agriculture can't compete. All the employers are in the same boat.

But in setting standards for pay the laird for many years now, certainly since the Second World War, has had to make sure that he pays his employees the same as, if not a little more than, the absolute minimum agricultural wage. This became the yardstick for measuring estate pay and it was the best thing that ever happened when the agricultural minimum came into force. From then on there was no need for a man to fear the despotic laird, the laird who was solely interested in

167

maintaining a large work force to ensure that his own life-style went on unhindered and unchanged. Asking for a rise in pay became a thing of the past. It just came to you automatically. Whenever the farm workers got it so, too, did the estate labourer, the forester, the gardener, the gamekeeper. The fear of causing trouble for yourself by going cap in hand to ask for a few more shillings was gone. Thank God. Because whether you got it or not all depended on how the laird was feeling that particular day you asked.

Now, this wasn't so bad if the laird was a decent man himself. He'd listen sympathetically. You might get your rise — you might not. But if he was a miserable fellow, or worse, someone who thought nothing of his workers and considered them all beneath him, then by doing this you were as good as standing up and declaring yourself a trouble-maker. What a disgusting way for a man to lead his life, always beholden to the whims and moods of another. There's none of that now and while, in a way, the old family feeling has gone from estates and with it much of the mutual respect between laird and worker, it is a much easier situation to be involved in. You work. You receive your wages. No more is expected of you. You expect no more from the laird. You can like or dislike him. It doesn't really matter. Your job is secure and not dependent on whims or temperament on his part.

I am a great believer in tradition; I like to preserve the continuity of things from the past, keep them alive in the present. I sometimes mourn the passing of the old times, miss the feeling and atmosphere there was on the estate when hordes of employees were around to keep the place running smoothly, looking after the house, the gardens, the grounds, the river, the moor. The place seemed more alive then. More homely in a way. But I have no regrets, no longing for the feudal outlook of the past, both by laird and employee. It caused too much bitterness and misery. Nine times out of ten the laird was a good man and it never caused any problems. However, there was always the tenth laird who made up for it in terms of upheaval and strife. Nowadays, it's much more a plain and simple job, just like any other job; more than a mere way of life to be slavishly followed by one generation after another.

Somehow, it's made life a lot more simple. A great deal of the worry has gone out of it. Oh yes, you'll hear the younger ones say that this thing is wrong and that thing is wrong, the money could be improved, the estate houses they're living in could be better maintained and modernized, that despite a new attitude to class among society throughout the country the lairds are still there in the upper classes looking down their noses at the workers struggling on below. This is a load of bloody nonsense. When someone speaks to me like this I just remind them that whatever your boss might think of you, or what you might think of him, even if you're not a first-class worker, you're safe from the fear of being sacked on the spot. That's something none of them has ever to worry about. It would be a rare happening indeed to come across any such thing taking place on an estate in the present day. In the past it happened all the time — in some places. The removal of this fear is the best thing that has happened in the whole of my working life on estates. You can still be dismissed, but if you are, then the laird or his factor has got to have reasons for doing so — and good ones at that.

This security has put new strength into the working man. He can look the laird straight in the eye and speak his mind as

169

a result of it. And if they're sensible — the lairds, that is — they'll listen to what the worker is saying, because in many cases they will be hearing the voice of experience — men who have developed skills in agriculture and forestry, in gardening like myself, and know what they're talking about. This sort of working man is just as deserving of respect from the present-day laird, who is much more of a businessman anyway, as his ancestors were deserving of respect because of the feudal nature of their hold over the workers in the past.

It's a changed way of life in many respects. New values. New ideas. There may be fewer estate workers running the place, but at least those who are can do so as independent beings, free from all ties of being in bond. That, to me, is worth a good deal more than most material benefits, such as high wages, things of this kind. It hasn't come about as a result of any long, hard struggle. Nothing like this. Indeed, on the face of things, there hardly appears to have been any struggle at all. It's just something that has gradually become part of estate life. Some of the older hands who can remember a lot further back than I can, may not like estate work being turned into a job just like any other. The old hands liked the mystique, the traditional role they were playing, father to son and all this sort of thing. Their pleasure came from being a part of this great tradition. It separated them from the ordinary working man outside the estate world. In certain ways they could be every bit as aloof as the laird when they wanted. They enjoyed being different. But not me. I'm quite happy to be part of the common herd.

I enjoy my job. I enjoy the surroundings in which I work. In the summer it's a lovely place and in the autumn there are so many different kinds of trees and shrubs that the whole place is one great mass of colour as the leaves change from green to brown, to red. In the winter it can be bitterly cold, with wind howling off the mountain, sleet, snow, frost, mist — you name it, we get it. But at this time of the year I always try to think of the spring only a few months away — and you know, before I realize what is happening, the first buds are on the trees, it's growing warmer and good times are here again.

I enjoy my job because I'm free to enjoy it. That's something my father could never have said. Perhaps, under the circumstances of his time, he was happy enough. I know I could never have been, having to work under his conditions. I like things the way they are now. Yes, I definitely think that, for the working man, an estate job is as good as any other today. The difference between now and then is quite simple. In the past you had to work on the estate if you lived in the area — or starve. Now, you just do it because you enjoy it. That counts for a hell of a lot in life.

CHAPTER
TWELVE

The old laundry at Strathalder stands forlorn and neglected, disused for more than twenty years and showing every sign of age and lack of maintenance. A clump of hazel bushes grows against one wall and close to the doorway a sprawling mass of deadly nightshade sprouts from the soil, growing higher and stronger with the passing of every year. The roof leaks where slates have slipped or been blown away by a gale; in summer several pairs of swallows nest in the rafters, coming and going through a missing window high in a gable wall.

It is hard to appreciate in the midst of such decay that this was, for many years, one of the busiest places on the estate — alive with activity from early morning to late at night when the mansion house was full of guests and the fishing and shooting seasons were under way. Every single thing that required to be washed was handled by the team of laundry maids and throughout the week a regular routine was enacted, with care and efficiency high on the list of everyone's priorities. The cook might be proud of the specialities which she created in her kitchen, but none was so proud as the head laundry maid at the sight of the crisp, starched sheets, ironed and folded, smelling clean and fragrant, ready for delivery at the end of a hard day's work. Not only were laundry maids expected to take pride in their work, but for their own peace of mind it was essential that they did so. Unlike some members of the estate and household staff who could perform their tasks without undue scrutiny, the laundry maids' handiwork was on constant display, looked at, handled and worn, not only by the laird and his wife and family, but by guests and other servants alike.

By the 1950s the laundry was considered to be a luxury item when it came to a ruthless pruning of costs, necessary in the face of mounting expenditure. The last laundry maid left, the door was closed and the considerably reduced amount of work to be done handed over for a number of years to an outside contractor. Now, as in the average home throughout the country, the Strathalder laundry is completed by a machine installed in a corner of the mansion house kitchen.

Janet Gray has particularly vivid memories of her days as a laundry maid. But before starting work on the estate on which she was born, she enjoyed, as a child during the years of the First World War, the friendship of the laird's young daughter. This, in addition to providing her with numerous childhood escapades, allowed her an early insight into the life-style of those who lived in the mansion house. Her father was one of the estate gardeners — and the laird's personal piper; an extra task which kept him busy both in the early morning and in the evening.

His first job each day was to play the bagpipes in order to waken the laird and his family at eight o'clock in the morning. Then, at eight o'clock every evening he had to play in the dining room. In the mornings he played his bagpipes as he marched up and down on the gravel path beneath their bedroom windows and in the evenings when they sat down to dine he would walk around the table at least three times, then continue playing in the passage outside the door.

Every day he had to write out his programme of tunes — what he was going to be playing that evening — and submit it to the laird for his approval. Sometimes he made changes, asked my father for some other tune. And when everyone sat down to dinner there was the list of tunes sitting on the dining table for all the guests to see. And God help my father if he ever forgot to submit his list of tunes in advance. The laird was a stickler for routine. It was the exact same ritual every day — three times around the table, then out and in and travel back and fore along the passage as they were eating.

He had to dress up for this performance, as well as for the one he did every morning, in kilt, green jacket, white shirt and tie. Around 7.30a.m. he left our cottage on the estate and walked up the drive to the Big House, where he played for half an hour, starting promptly at eight o'clock. Then he came back home, ate his breakfast and changed into ordinary working clothes, ready to do his day's work as a gardener. He finished the gardening at five o'clock in the afternoon, came home, had his supper and a bath, got dressed once again in all the regalia, collected his bagpipes and was back at the Big House a few minutes before eight o'clock when they always sat down to dine. He would stay there for about an hour, playing usually until nine o'clock, then he was free to come home again.

For this he received 1s.6d. a week extra on top of his gardener's wages of £2 a week. He did this in all weathers, at all times of the year — day in, day out. I'd say without fear of contradiction that the laird got his money's-worth; a first-class personal piper for only 1s.6d. a week.

Dinner was always prompt at eight o'clock in the evening. There would be anything from eight to forty people, depending, whether it was just a family affair or a dinner party for guests staying in the house and others invited from neighbouring estates. There was a great deal of entertaining went on, especially when the grouse and pheasant shooting was in progress and many dinner parties were held with lots of young people invited.

The butler and footmen would be in attendance, right, left and centre and the head steward. He was responsible for all manner of things, including when to give the piper the nod that it was time for him to proceed into the dining room. Just before one particular dinner party I happened to be allowed in to see the dining room before the guests arrived. As far as I was concerned it was like being given a peep at another world from the one I lived in. There were long, trailing flowers hanging down, right along the middle of the room from end to end and all the silver glittered on the huge white cloth which was laid over the most enormous table I'd ever seen.

I was about eight years old at the time — this was in 1917 — and on that evening I believe thirty-six were going to sit down to dinner. I was amazed by the amount of cutlery, knives, forks and spoons all in their correct places. I'd never seen so many things lying on a table before this. I was, to put

175

it mildly, completely astonished that there should be so much. I was fascinated by the wine glasses — something I'd never seen before. Although I didn't know it at the time, of course, the glasses were of the most expensive crystal, but to me they were like rows of twinkling stars with the lights from the chandeliers above the table reflected in them. The butler was there, walking the length of the table, stopping now and then to bend over to straighten a knife or a napkin. He seemed to be a very solemn man, tall and straight, severe-looking in his black clothes.

I was with the daughter of the house who was ten years old, two years older than me, and too young to be attending the dinner party. We were always together, playing around the house or in the grounds and gardens. We got up to a great deal of mischief and had lots of fun, and being kids, it never entered our heads to question our different status in life — me, the daughter of the gardener and she, the daughter of the laird with that fine house and all that land and employing so many people, my own father included. We were just friends, playmates, and happily our friendship continued into adult life without a single trace of any difference making itself felt.

If there was any finer place than this for a child to be brought up so that he or she had no class consciousness in their nature, then I've never come across it. Her mother was a wee bit of a snob, but the laird himself — well, it didn't seem to matter to him whether a person was a cowman or a count. He treated everybody alike and spoke to them in similar fashion. He was a model of courtesy and expected the same behaviour in return.

So, being privileged in a way to be so close to the daughter, this was my first sight of one of the grand dinner parties I'd heard so much about. When it was time for the guests to enter we both went up a side stair in the main hall and had a good view of the men and their ladies going into the dining room. I must have been staring goggle-eyed through the rails on the landing watching the women in all their finery, beautiful gowns and a fair sprinkling of diamonds and other expensive jewellery distributed among them.

Then, when we saw them all go in and the door was shut we were off like two hares to see what we could scrounge. There was no point in going to the kitchen because the cook was too busy to be bothered with the likes of us, so we went to the gardens. Peaches, grapes, tomatoes — plenty of good things were there for us to eat. And if none of the gardeners were around to give us what we wanted, then we just went into the greenhouses and helped ourselves. Like most children, we were always hungry and provided we didn't get in the way the cook would allow us into her kitchen and never failed to find us something to eat. The same went for the gardeners. But it was an unwritten law that we would never say we had been given anything and they would never tell the lady of the house that we — or, at least her own daughter — had been filling up with cake or fruit between meals. It was a form of conspiracy — something that gave both sides a great deal of pleasure and fun. It was a game we all shared.

I remember one occasion when we were both in the kitchen being given a big sandwich each by the cook when footsteps were heard approaching along the passage. It was her ladyship making an unexpected call. Normally, she only ever appeared in the kitchen once a day, always at the same time, around ten o'clock in the morning.

Mary, the daughter, had no wish to be caught by her mother eating between meals (something her mother was continually warning her about doing) and neither had I any desire to receive the sharp edge of her tongue. So, Mary ran across the kitchen and squeezed herself into a cupboard where the brooms and scrubbing brushes were kept. One of the kitchen maids shut the door firmly behind her. But I had no time to get there. Luckily, I was standing beside a huge barrel used for storing salt, so I lifted the lid and jumped inside. Quick as a flash the cook thumped the lid down and I was left there in the dark, up to my knees in salt. I don't know how long went past while I was stuck inside the salt barrel; it seemed like an eternity. All the while I could hear her ladyship's voice droning on and now and then the cook replying with some comment or other. I do know that I was terrified in case I might make a noise; that I might sneeze or do something silly like that. Anyway, eventually her ladyship departed and once she was safely through the door and there was no sign of her returning, the cook lifted the lid to release me. When I clambered out on to the floor the first thing I noticed, apart from my shoes being filled with grains of salt, was that my sandwich was ruined. It was absolutely covered in salt. I expect the cook saw the look of disappointment on my face because she said right away, "Throw that thing on the fire and I'll make you up another one." And she did. An even bigger and better sandwich than the first one.

When I started work as a laundry maid I felt really proud to be getting a job connected with the estate. To me, it was the greatest place on earth. All estates had their own laundry. On some it was huge, depending, of course, on the overall size of the entire establishment; some had as many as eight or nine laundry maids. The usual figure for an estate the size of this one — a typically average size of estate — was between three and five.

The laundry was housed in a big building alongside the wall of the main garden, with a large drying-green to one side where all the things were hung out on lines to get them dry when the weather was fine. What a great sight it was on a really good day, with the wind blowing, to see the lines full with the laundry and it flapping and cracking in the breeze. And such a good, clean scent was in the air — of fresh soap and water. It's something I'll never forget — that clean, pure smell from something that's been washed in soap, then hung in the open air to dry. All your modern detergents and washing powders, your fancy machines and spin-driers, can never achieve this. They may get the clothes clean. Oh yes, they'll manage this. But they'll never get them to smell good — and clean. Not like I remember how things smelt there on the drying-green at the end of a long, hard day sweating from the heat thrown out by the washing tubs.

Inside the laundry building there were a number of rooms. The main one was where all the washing was done in wooden tubs — great monsters of things — placed all around the walls. Next to this was the drying room, where the laundry was hung up to dry during the winter months or, as seemed to happen so often, when the weather was wet during the summer and use of the drying-green was ruled out. The other main room — a long, narrow room — was the ironing room where we all worked with heavy facing irons heated from a big stove in the centre of the floor. In the summer, even with the windows wide open, this was a dreadfully hot room in which to work, although the washing room itself took a bit of beating when it came to heat.

With the stove on full blast to heat the water in the boilers and all the tubs full, with the steam gushing out like smoke, it was like being in one of those greenhouses where they raise tropical plants. And in addition to this we had to carry the hot water in buckets and empty it into the tubs, so whatever the temperature was like, inside or out, you soon worked up a fine heat yourself with all this carrying to and fro; fetching the buckets, stirring the contents of the tubs with long, wooden poles, draining the water off the tubs and emptying it out, refilling them in order to rinse.

We were all quite young girls — I'd have been sixteen or seventeen when I started work in the laundry — so although we weren't great hefty types we were fit — and tough. We had to be, to stand the pace. And if you weren't tough when you started, then it wasn't long before you were. Or else you left to try something less energetic. There were five of us for a time, including the head laundry maid. I still went on living at home in our house on the estate, but the others had their living quarters above the main building — kitchen, bathroom, sitting room and bedrooms. Then, in the mid-1920s, 1925 or 1926 or thereabouts, the laundry staff was cut back to three and the other two girls were given rooms in the servants' wing of the Big House and took their meals with the rest of the staff.

At first, for a time after I started work, washing was done every day — except Sunday; two or three of us would be doing this while the others were catching up on the ironing of the previous batch. There was always plenty to do — never a dull or an idle moment. Hampers of dirty linen would arrive at the door, brought to us by one of the gardeners driving a pony and cart. When the house was full of guests, as it so often was during the shooting season, or when the salmon fishing was at its best, there was a huge amount of laundry to be done. And not only clothes, but towels, sheets and pillowcases and enormous white tablecloths, white napkins and the like; all the fol-de-rols of the day. When I speak of them being white I really mean white, not the sort of greyish-white look about things that so often passes for white today. For a time there was a housekeeper at the Big House who was, in herself, a kind enough soul, but most certainly a person who had standards; high standards. And among those standards was a belief that the tablecloths must be pristine white. Nothing less would satisfy her. So our head laundry maid always took extra care to supervise us girls when it came to the washing of the table-cloths or else she would take them herself and see to it personally that when they emerged from the wash they might be even whiter than the day they had been new and first bought.

The laundry catered for everyone, those living in the Big House, family, guests and servants as well as all the single men living in the bothy. Their sheets, just like everyone else's in the servants' quarters, were great, heavy double sheets changed once a week. At one time there were nine men living in the bothy so even with their washing, not counting around forty living in the Big House, you can well imagine the tremendous amount of work that had to be done — and done well, not once, but all the time.

Later, when staff members were cut, we stopped washing every day. Instead, it was done on Mondays, Tuesdays and Wednesdays, when the chauffeur had to light the boiler fires

181

so that we could get on with the work. For the rest of the week we attended to the drying-off and the ironing. It was all tough, hard work — every minute of it. But we never thought of it as being menial work. We took a pride in doing it well. This provided us with fresh interest every day. Our one aim in life was to do the next lot of laundry better than we had managed the previous lot. We were aiming for excellence. It was expected of us. So, in order to lead a contented life, we jolly well made sure that they got it. Everybody. From the laird right down to the rawest apprentice gardener straight out of school.

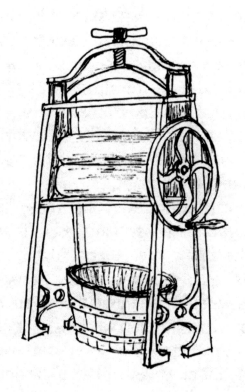

CHAPTER
THIRTEEN

In rural Scotland, wherever there are estates, either large or small, the factor is a figure performing a role every bit as traditional as the laird. The factor is, in effect, the laird's managing director, his confidant, the person responsible for the smooth administration of the estate. Everything, from paying the wages and salaries of employees to arranging the letting of salmon fishing, deer stalking and grouse shooting, passes through his hands and comes under his scrutiny. He is an important figure in the life of an estate — on some he is held in more esteem, in greater awe, or even with more hostility, than the laird himself. Next to the laird he holds the position of real power and in many cases, where the estate is owned by a syndicate or by someone who does not live on the property, the factor is the only arbiter of disputes, the sole figure of influence, of authority, with whom employees and tenants can deal.

Factors — the bad ones at least — have earned for themselves a special place in Scottish history, in particular with regard to that tragic period in the nineteenth century known as the Highland Clearances, when, in places, entire villages were abandoned as lairds made way for sheep in place of the people whose ancestors had always inhabited the glens and the straths. The influx of sheep was to make many a laird a wealthy man, but for those who were harried and chased from their homes, many of them to emigrate to Canada and the United States of America, there was nothing but sustained hardship and misery. Most notorious of all the factors was Patrick Sellar, who administered the Duke of Sutherland's estates and in June, 1814, burnt the village of Strathnaver around the heads of its inhabitants in a determined and successful attempt to evict them. As his men went from house to house firing the buildings, he was heard to announce, "The devil a man of them, sick or well, shall remain."

The inhuman behaviour of Sellar and others like him soured the image of the factor for many years to come. At the same time it served to strengthen his position of power so that on Highland estates he became a figure of immense influence. All the same, any deference shown to him by the tenants and employees of a laird was offered more in fear than from respect, due to his status in the community. However, in late Victorian times, he was to lose much of his autocratic power due to a greater degree of benevolence on the part of many lairds and, perhaps more pertinently, because certain laws had been strengthened more in favour of the common man, which left him shorn of the trappings of absolute dictator over the lives of the laird's people.

In the 1920s and up to the end of the Second World War Strathalder, in common with many large estates, had a resident factor permanently around the place dealing solely with the affairs of the one estate.

Nowadays this is an indulgence few lairds can afford; only on several extremely large establishments. Modern estate management is now in the hands of the freelance factor — a man who has several estates in his care and who divides his time and his loyalty among a number of lairds, each one receiving a degree of attention proportionate to the size of the estate. But despite this change the scope of his job remains very much the same. The modern factor must be just as conversant with a variety of wide-ranging matters, from law to the cost of building materials, as his resident counterpart from the past. He must be sage and prophet, counsellor and judge, depending on the circumstances and the mood of the moment. In the past he was held in awe whether or not he was liked by those over whom he held sway. Today, this status is no longer accorded him, but at all levels on the estate he is treated with respect; for when you talk to the factor, you are, in effect, talking to the shadow of the laird.

Martin Farquharson is the factor for several estates of varying size. It is a way of life that first appealed to him as a boy on an estate when he would see the resident factor and be left in no doubt that here was "a most important person".

My father having been a tenant farmer during the whole of his working life, I was brought up on an estate and in an environment where everyone regarded the factor as being one of the most important figures in the community. I am looking back to the days of my youth, around sixty years ago, and what is still a vivid recollection to me is that the laird remained very much aloof from his tenants and employees, and the factor was the man who really mattered.

Such an estate provided a source of livelihood for upwards of one hundred families or thereabouts. Apart from the usual outdoor staff of foresters, gardeners, gamekeepers and gillies, all classes of tradesmen were also employed to deal with maintenance work and in many instances throughout Scotland villages became established where the majority of the male population worked on and lived in cottages belonging to the estate. This was the position on the estate of my boyhood years and in such a society it is therefore not too hard to visualize that the factor was an extremely important person who was looked up to with respect and at the same time held in very high regard by all those who came in contact with him. As a youngster I can well remember his commanding figure, invariably in Highland dress, driving around with his pony and trap. This mode of transport was soon to be replaced by a motor car, complete with chauffeur, which in those far-off days was a source of wonderment and, naturally, further enhanced his standing among the local people.

This image of life as an estate factor must have created a very favourable impression on my young mind and while it was my original intention to follow my father's footsteps in farming, agriculture was suffering from such a severe depression during the late twenties and early thirties, that I decided to take up factoring as a career. I served my apprenticeship in the office of a factor who managed a number of estates in Central Scotland, starting work on an annual salary of £30. With modest yearly increments of £20 it

186

was quite a number of years before I ceased to be a burden on my parents.

However, at the age of twenty-eight, I applied for and was fortunate to secure the appointment as resident factor on an estate which, although relatively small, comprised a number of valuable arable farms, hill grazings, a productive grouse moor and fairly extensive woodlands. The owner, who had other business interests, was seldom in residence and this gave me a wonderful opportunity to have a fairly free hand in the day-to-day management of the property. Sadly, the sudden and untimely death of the proprietor necessitated part of the estate being sold and this prompted me to try to establish myself as a non-resident factor on a number of small estates which did not justify the employment of a full-time agent.

My reasons for taking this step were two-fold. First of all, the ever-increasing burden of taxation was leading to the breaking-up of many of the larger Scottish estates and the prospects of securing a really worthwhile resident factorship were becoming few and far between. Secondly, I considered — and rightly so, as the events of the past years have proved — that I would have a far greater degree of independence with several properties to manage rather than having my life bound up with one place that could one day cease to exist as an entire estate.

As was only to be expected the first few years were rather lean ones, but gradually additional business did come along and the step I took is one which I have never regretted. It has meant a most interesting and varied career. I think it can be said with a certain degree of truth that an estate factor requires to be a "Jack of all trades." A knowledge of the law

187

on all matters pertaining to the ownership and tenancy of land and sporting subjects is essential. Practical experience of farming, which enables one to talk the same language and appreciate the problems of farm tenants, is also highly desirable. A sound knowledge of all the building trades and costs is a must and while a factor need not be an architect in the full sense of the word, the ability to draw simple plans is a decided advantage. Other requirements are a sound knowledge of silviculture and, to a lesser extent, gardening; taxation too, in so far as this affects landed estates and the letting of agricultural land and all types of sporting subjects, including salmon fishing and also house property.

In the early 1930s the wages paid to the heads of departments — forestry, gamekeeping and gardening — were around thirty-six shillings a week, with free house, two loads of firewood a year and an allowance of milk at one penny per pint. The grieve on the Home Farm received a few shillings more, with allowances of potatoes and meal. I can remember engaging a general farm worker for the princely sum of £40 in the half year, plus a free house, meal, milk and potatoes. The strange thing is that they all appeared to manage and I'm fairly certain that despite particular hardships they were probably more contented with their lives than many farm workers of the present day.

In those days a good price for a 10 cwt prime fat bullock was considered to be around £20, Blackface wether lambs fetched in the region of 23s per head, while oats and barley realized about 14s per quarter; all prices that bear absolutely no comparison with those of today.

On the subject of farm rents it's safe to say that the land on this estate can be considered as average. The pre-war average rent was approximately 15s per acre, with rent revisions due only at fairly long intervals. The present figure is £7 per acre. There have been few tenancy changes in recent years and there is no doubt that if any of the farms were available to let on the open market, very substantially higher rents could be obtained. One typical upland estate which I factored for a number of years and similar to this one extended to approximately four thousand acres and comprised some six let farms which consisted of very moderate arable land with rough grazing outruns. These produced a total rental of around £700 per annum. There was also a small grouse moor, plus salmon fishing from one bank of a river, which formed the boundary of the property, but the most valuable feature was the quite extensive woodlands. The staff consisted of four foresters, two gamekeepers, three gardeners and one joiner/handyman who was qualified to deal with most types of maintenance work, provided these were not of a major nature. The average weekly wage of these employees was around £2, representing an annual total outlay of just over £1000. The present-day outlay for the same number of employees, including the employer's share of National Insurance, would be fully £25,000.

On a small estate the sources of revenue to meet such vastly increased overheads are very limited and the staff employed in non-productive departments, such as private gardens, has had to be drastically cut down. Modern mechanical equipment and the use of weed-killers have, of course, considerably reduced the amount of manual labour required and with cutting out some of the frills and extravagances, one man should now be able to satisfactorily look after the same extent of gardens and grounds which took up the time of three men thirty to forty years ago. If an estate is within easy reach of a centre of population, a ready market can usually be found for surplus garden produce and properly managed market gardening has, in many instances, become a source of additional revenue.

There are few estate owners now who can afford not to let at least part of their sporting rights and in recent years there has been a vastly increased demand for grouse and low ground shooting, stalking and salmon fishing. This upsurge of interest stems not only from people in this country, but particularly so from those on the Continent. In the immediate pre-war and post-war years it is probably not far off the mark to suggest that grouse shooting rents would have been based on £1 per brace, stalking at £10 per stag and salmon fishing at £2 per fish on the previous five-year average records. Over the years these figures have continued to rise and present-day rates can probably be fairly quoted, depending on the quality of sport offered, at £10 per brace for grouse, £65 per head for stags (with the estate retaining the venison) and £30 to £35 per salmon.

In one of my old cash books there is the following entry: "August 25, 1934 — Proceeds of sale of 394 grouse and one plover — £27.3s." This represents an income of rather less than 7.5p per bird. The present price obtained for young grouse at the beginning of the season on August 12 is around £1 per bird, which seems low compared with the price of £3.20 being charged a few days later for the same birds in some London stores.

The price received for venison in pre-war days was no more than a few old pence per pound in weight, if it was sold at all. Most of it was given away. In 1967 the figure was 2s.2d, but it has risen dramatically since then to reach an average of 73p. This means that the carcase value of a good stag is between £100 and £110, to which has to be added the rent of £65 received from the party who has had the pleasure of stalking the beast. In 1976 on one estate I am associated with, the income from stag and hind venison amounted to fully £13,500. Now, with the increased price and with roughly the same number of animals being killed, the income is around £16,500. While this income might seem a considerable figure it must be borne in mind that the wages outlay in respect of two full-time stalkers, plus seasonal gillies, amounts to approximately £7000. In addition the rateable value of deer forests has risen substantially over the years and will no doubt do so again at the next re-valuation. All the same it is probably fair to say that the ownership of a really productive deer forest is the best capital investment there is in the sporting world; this is reflected in the prices which have recently been paid for such forests — £750,000 and thereabouts for six to seven thousand acres of land. Commercial deer farming is now being practised on some estates, but the initial outlay on fencing must obviously be substantial and the cost of feeding the beasts in severe weather is an expensive item.

Salmon fishing has become increasingly popular during the past thirty years and estates which have been fortunate enough to retain the ownership of fishing during this period have enjoyed very considerable capital appreciation. One stretch of fishing on a well-known river was sold some twenty-five years ago at a price based on a capital value of just under £100 per salmon. Two or three years ago a price of £1000 per fish was obtained, but this has now fallen back a little and stabilized itself at around £700 per fish, which is considered to be a realistic figure. Even although rents have risen enormously during the past ten years or so the ownership of recently purchased fishing cannot be considered as a worthwhile revenue-producing investment in relation to the capital tied up; all that can be hoped for in such circumstances is further capital appreciation. Whether this will be forthcoming is anyone's guess and in any case capital gains tax lurks around the corner.

In 1949 a short stretch of rather moderate fishing on one of the less renowned rivers was being let on a seasonal basis at a rent of £25. The rent of this fishing on the same basis is now £350 and if the owner cared to go to the trouble of arranging short-term weekly or fortnightly lets, a higher figure could no doubt be obtained. Around twenty years ago I knew one tenant who rented fishing on a very productive river on the agreement that he paid £5 for every fish caught. During the month of July, when there was a very good run of small grilse, with a sale value of around ten shillings each, I remember him telling me jocularly that he tried to shake them off the hook rather than debit himself with yet another £5. By the early 1960s rents were being charged at £10 per fish on the average records for the previous five years and this rate has continued to increase — the present day figure being around £35 per fish. This has been necessary in order to meet rising outlays on gillies' wages, rates, Fishery Board assessments, river bank and boat maintenance, together with other administrative costs which, unfortunately, have caused some people to adopt a much more commercially-minded attitude to what should be regarded as a sport. All the same this is not altogether surprising when fresh spring salmon can fetch up to and around £2.50 per lb.

On an estate where an owner in pre-war days had the foresight to turn over what was otherwise unproductive land to forestry, he is now reaping the benefit of revenue and an ever-increasing capital asset. This has enabled him to continue employing the same forestry staff, although nowadays the staff on many estates must be prepared to undertake additional duties such as vermin destruction and seasonal farm work when things are slack in their own particular department. Costs of timber products have, like everything else, increased dramatically. In pre-war days a twelve foot long fencing rail cost one shilling and a five foot post was only ninepence. The present-day charges are 80p and 64p respectively. I well remember when it was possible to engage a contractor to erect a fence comprising six strands of wire for threepence a yard, with the estate supplying the material. The present-day cost for simply erecting the fence is at least 18p per yard. The cost of general repairs and improvements to estate buildings has also risen substantially in recent years. When I'm faced with seemingly enormous charges my mind goes back to 1938 and an estimate I received for the picking and re-pointing of all the external walls on a very sizeable mansion house. It amounted to just on £300. It is probably fair to say that the same work today would cost at least £3000.

I have already mentioned the outdoor staff employed on a large estate and how their numbers have been reduced. But the greatest change, to my mind, has come about in connection with staff responsible for the running of the laird's residence, be it castle or large mansion house. Some fifty or more years ago the permanent staff in a large establishment would have consisted of a butler, two or three footmen, a housekeeper, with probably four or five parlour maids and chamber maids, and a chef or cook with at least a couple of kitchen maids. In addition there would be the laundry staff and in a few places the estate even had its own bakery and slaughter house. Added to this number were the coachmen — probably two or three — to be replaced with chauffeurs with the advent of the motor car. Now, of course, most of these jobs have disappeared entirely, cost being one reason, but mainly due to the changes that have come about in the general structure of society.

Following the war years ever-increasing taxation began to make itself felt and this gradually resulted in the breaking-up of the really large estates throughout the country. The portions offered for sale were usually purchased by people who had other business interests and it is probably true to say that the great majority of the small estates are now owned by such people. Even so, it has been necessary to become much more commercially-minded in order to make ends meet. And this applies whether or not the estate is primarily seen as a form of investment on the part of its owner or as a home first, and investment second. The letting of sporting rights is now commonplace, with the owner only retaining such periods in the year as he can afford to absent himself from his other business commitments. The really large residences have become holiday homes, so to speak, with only temporary staff being employed. Some are run on the lines of an hotel, to provide accommodation for sporting tenants, while others of historic interest are now on view to the general public, with the owner reserving only a few apartments for his own private use. Another venture in this modern age has been the establishment of caravan parks and these last two developments have produced substantial additional income, at the same time providing a useful source of employment for local people.

On an estate on which I was employed in pre-war days and where the mansion house was more or less permanently occupied, it was written into all the farm leases that the tenants had annually to provide horse and cart transport for the driving of coal from the nearest railway station to the mansion house. This had to be done on a set day each year and it was quite a sight to see a convoy of around thirty horses and carts on the public road and winding its way up the long drive. In those days good quality coal cost around £1.15s. per ton compared with today's figure of £48 or £50 for the same amount.

On moving up from central Scotland to the north-east I initially experienced a little difficulty in understanding some of the local dialect. One day a tenant farmer called at my office with the request that he would like permission "to cut some sprots for thecking his strae soos". Not wishing to show my ignorance, a few guarded questions were required before I was able to establish that he wished to cut rushes for the purpose of thatching his straw stacks. On another occasion, when I was engaging an employee, he asked for permission to keep a few hens "as an egg was aye handy to have about the hoose". I agreed to this and it was written into his contract of employment that he would be allowed to have not more than ten head of poultry with provision for keeping these on a small area of rough ground behind his cottage. Some time later the grieve from the Home Farm informed me that this employee was helping himself to oats from the grain-loft and naturally I decided that this practice had to be stopped. When I spoke to the man he maintained that according to his agreement he was entitled to food for his poultry and although I assured him that this was not the case he did not appear to be completely convinced. A few days later, when I had occasion to call at his house, his wife, who was a most formidable woman and inclined to wear the trousers, thrust an open dictionary into my face and said, "Look! Provision means food." In the future I was extremely careful about the wording of such contracts of employment.

What was for me a slightly embarrassing situation cropped up on one occasion when I was going to visit one of my lairds and he kindly suggested that I should spend the night in the mansion house. He made the further suggestion that unless I wished to travel light I should pack a dinner jacket and black tie as his house party always dressed for dinner. After dining and wining well I eventually got off to bed rather late and stepping out of my clothes I left them, probably rather untidily, on a bedroom chair. Next morning a knock on my door heralded the butler with a cup of tea and he then proceeded to pick up my dinner-suit and took it away for pressing. I thought to myself, "Oh my God. What on earth will he find in the pockets?" A few minutes later he reappeared bearing a silver salver on which lay an assortment of loose change, golf tees, pieces of paper and other odds and ends. All I could do was mumble something to the effect that I was not accustomed to such personal service. Being a good servant, the butler merely smiled politely and withdrew.

Provided one enjoys shooting and fishing, these are two of the fringe benefits of being an estate factor, the only problem being to find the time to accept all the invitations that come along from both the lairds and their tenants. One popular activity many years ago — and something in which everybody took part no matter whether they were laird or worker — was curling. This was before the establishment of indoor ice-rinks and if a laird was keen on "the roaring game", all employees on the estate who could throw a stone would be ordered to down tools and report to the curling pond on any day when conditions were right. There were many such days at that time because the winters were much more severe up here than they normally are now — weeks of snow and frost. It was extremely enjoyable and as a result most estate employees became very interested and highly proficient at the game to which work was considered of secondary importance.

In the days before the ownership of cars became a commonplace feature of life and travelling further afield was made easy, many estate owners did much in the way of providing social amenities in the country districts in which their estates were situated. This helped to foster a true community spirit and it meant that the local people had activities which they could enjoy no matter how isolated or remote the area in which they lived. Lairds donated handsomely towards the cost of building village halls, indoor rifle ranges and sports grounds. They did it because they saw a need for such things. And the locals, estate workers and others alike, responded by using them and enjoying the facilities. In most places where there was a hall there was barely an evening went past during the winter months without it being used for a meeting, a concert, a dance or a whist drive. Young and old alike mingled freely — there was little sign of any generation gap between them — and I'm sure it's right to say that everyone, no matter their family and financial circumstances, enjoyed a happier and more contented social life at that time than is the case today. On most modern estates the spirit of community has vanished completely. It is, quite definitely, something that belongs entirely to the past.

CHAPTER
FOURTEEN

The popular image of a gamekeeper as being a man who walks around the estate all day with a gun under his arm and an obedient dog at his heel is a view that has been prevalent for many years. Most likely this myth grew and took hold as a result of other estate workers seeing what, to them, was the comparative freedom of the gamekeeper's life as distinct from their own regulated and supervised conditions of employment. But what they — and others who live in the countryside — often fail to understand is the necessity for the gamekeeper to work alone and without someone checking his every movement and the fact that in order to do his job properly, as regards control of vermin and keeping poachers at bay, it is essential for him to be seen to be doing it. If he is working hard and being conscientious then he will always be somewhere within the bounds of the estate on any particular day of the week; and the basic tools of his trade are a gun and a good dog.

Perhaps more than any other job on the estate, gamekeeping is the one most rooted in tradition, sons following fathers in the role of protector of the laird's shooting and fishing interests, destroyer of the predators who feed on the pheasants and grouse, guardian of all animals and birds whose presence provides an opportunity to further the sporting interests of the estate. By tradition gamekeepers are, invariably, silent, solitary men. They have to be; the nature of their job demands a deep and total rapport with the countryside in which they work. They must be as effective in blending with the background as the creatures they hunt, as cunning and as quick-witted as their prey.

As the pattern of life on Strathalder and similar estates has changed in recent years so, too, has the gamekeeper been forced to adapt and conform to a different emphasis being placed on his work. In the 1920s all shooting and fishing carried out on the estate was for the sole pleasure of the laird and his invited guests. Nine gamekeepers shared the burden of ensuring that the laird was given every opportunity to pursue his favourite pastime and in turn their employer spared no expense to see that the game department was given priority in all matters. Now, although the present laird is still an accomplished master of the shotgun and an experienced fisherman, it is no longer possible for him to indulge himself to the same extent in the endless pursuit of enjoyment practised by his ancestors. Two gamekeepers now do the work of his father's nine and today the emphasis is on attracting the paying sporting enthusiast, of whom there are many, willing to part with considerable sums of money for the opportunity of participating in a grouse or pheasant shoot.

But for the true gamekeeper — the man who sees his job as a way of life and not merely the means of making money — the old traditions die hard. He has managed to salvage something from the past so that he can maintain and keep alive the standards which, above all else, stamped his estate with its considerable reputation among sporting men. Whether they are paying for their sport, as they do now, or, as in the past, enjoying themselves by personal invitation, the sportsman will find himself in the company of a unique and distinctive breed of countryman. The gamekeeper's job can be a lonely, difficult and often thankless one. But whether born to do it in the family tradition or a newcomer who has chosen the job in order to lead an open-air life, dedication is present in the majority of those who tackle it.

In his book, *The Gamekeeper at Home*, published in 1878, Richard Jeffries wrote, "To make a good keeper it requires not only honesty and skill, but a considerable amount of 'backbone' in the character to resist temptation and to control subordinates. The keeper who has gone to the bad becomes one of the most mischievous members of the community: the faithful and upright keeper is not only a valuable servant, but a protection to all kinds of property."

In the opinion of head gamekeeper Neil Mackay, those qualities, remarked on a century ago, are still the prime requirements if any gamekeeper — young or old — is to make a success both of his life and in the running of the game department on the estate. Now close to retirement, he has seen the world of the

Strathalder gamekeeper — both working and social life — subjected to the ever-increasing pressure of change; some which he welcomes, others he could well do without.

Before leaving school it was always my ambition to be a gamekeeper. And many a knock on the ears I got from the teacher because I'd be sitting at my desk day-dreaming, elbows on the desk, gazing into space, thinking about setting traps or snares somewhere. Most of the young fellows and the girls, too, who lived around the estate were fairly sure of getting a job on the estate when their school days were over. You booked up well in advance; say, like me, you wanted to be a gamekeeper, then the first step was to become a kennel boy, doing all the odd jobs around the place in addition to looking after the dogs. So you put your name down well in advance and whenever a vacancy occurred after you left school you were taken on to start work. There was always a long waiting list — lots of people after a few jobs. So, when you got a job you had to look after it in order to keep it.

However, for the first year or so after I left school at the age of fourteen — in the mid 1920s — I had to work on a farm until a place could be found for me in the game department. Well, as regards farm work — it was detestable to me. Not that I minded hard work. No, to be free of the school and working outdoors, in good weather or bad, was something I had longed for. But on the farm I found myself doing endless jobs which I found monotonous and wearisome because whether it's hard work or easy work there's no fun in it if the hours you spend doing it are filled with boredom. I longed to escape, spent my days at work thinking about it and my nights dreaming of it.

My chance came during the grouse shooting season which begins every year on August 12. I was hired to go as a beater and right from the start found myself enjoying every moment of my new temporary job. Now, for anyone who doesn't know what a beater does, it involves being part of a long line of men (well in my young days it was mostly all men though now quite a few women take part) advancing spread out across the face of a particular part of the moor, waving sticks with coloured flags attached to them. The aim is to make the grouse, lying low among the tussocks of heather, rise up and fly off towards and over the guns, waiting hidden in the butts, constructions of stone or netting wire faced with turf and heather so that they are camouflaged with the background. It may sound like a jolly easy day's work, all this walking about and waving of flags. But believe me, nothing could be further from the truth. You have to keep position with the beater on either side of you, but take your pace not from him but from the man on the flank, usually the head gamekeeper himself or one of his more experienced under-keepers, sometimes a trusted and reliable beater from former years. Well, apart from keeping in line and keeping up with what is sometimes a fast pace, you are expected to go straight ahead whether it's easy walking on solid moorland with nothing but the stalks of heather at your ankles or fording a burn in full spate or crossing a marshland, sometimes up to your waist in sticky, slimy mud. Yes, I've been there on the moor at grouse shooting time in all weathers and whatever my job in the proceedings as the years went past, I always enjoyed myself. Yes, even when times were bad and things were going wrong for some reason or other, when I'd sit down and put my feet up in the evening I'd think to myself, "Well, life's not so bad after all — whatever the sport is like, however difficult the problems." You see, I found I was completely and utterly at home out there on the open moor. I was at one with the sights and the sounds; and the fresh air, no matter how bitter the wind, always seemed to be pure and clean. Wholesome, that's the best word to describe it.

Well, after my first season as a beater it made me more determined than ever to become a gamekeeper. I can still remember the mood of depression that came over me when the shooting was finished and it was back to the farm for me — cleaning out the cow byre, chopping up frozen turnips to feed the beasts during the winter months, chipping the ice out of the drinking troughs. And all the time there beyond the fields I could see the uplands start to rise and the moor spread out across the skyline. And I wanted to be up there, tramping across it, among the chattering cries of the grouse that remained and the whooping of the lapwings as they wheeled around, floating above the cotton grass where in the spring they would make their nests.

Anyhow, the great day eventually arrived and I was able to start work as a kennel boy. I had to cook great quantities of porridge and make it really thick. This meant standing over the boiler with a long, thick pole, stirring and stirring the bubbling contents until the mass became so thick the piece of wood could stand upright and not fall over. I had to be extremely careful not to burn or singe the porridge otherwise the head gamekeeper was quick to give me the sharp edge of his tongue. When the porridge was ready I scooped it out

204

into a large trough and when it set it was ready to cut into sections for feeding to the dogs. I also had to cook rabbits and hares and every day I was doing something in the boiler.

In the old days it was mostly grouse shooting, but eventually pheasant rearing was started in the north here, after it was found how successful it was in England. This made a tremendous difference to the standard of sport on the estates and increased the stock to such an extent that pheasant shooting on a large scale became a common feature of estate life by the early 1930s.

Nowadays, the rearing of pheasant chicks to maturity — from the hatching of the eggs through to the day when the first shoot of the season takes place — is a much simpler and cleaner business than it was when it first started. Like so many other things in life today machines have taken over and all the egg hatching is controlled by incubators, followed by the placing of the chicks in electrically heated brooders. Then, when they first go into the open air they are in special enclosures, kept warm and dry by heaters, usually powered by bottled gas. One man can comfortably look after thousands of chicks, whereas in my young days to rear the same amount would have required several men and boys working at all hours of the day and night, battling against the weather, an army of predators from stoats and weasels to hawks, as well as a variety of diseases and ailments which young pheasants are prone to catch.

Yes, the early methods of doing this job were very primitive compared with what goes on now. For a start, all the chicks were reared by broody hens. You started to prepare by getting all the brood boxes together in one place and making hollows in pieces of turf which you placed in each box so that the hen could sit down comfortably. When these were ready it was time to go around all the farms on the estate and collect the broody hens — as many as you could possibly lay your hands on. This had to be done at night when they were roosting so it meant a good deal of poking around in the dark with torches flashing on and off as you grabbed the individual broody birds and placed them in a sack. Every nest you had prepared was filled with china eggs — dummy eggs as we called them — and each hen was placed on these in the nests. Again, this was done in the dark. Every hen had also to be tagged so that you knew which farm it belonged to when the time came to return them all when the rearing season was over. Of course hens were very cheap then, so there was no problem in getting them from the farmers.

The pheasant eggs, some from the wild, but mostly bought in from a pheasant farm in the south, were hatched off in paraffin heated incubators. They demanded constant attention, to see they didn't go out or start smoking. Then,

when the hatching got underway hens and chicks were put together in coops set out in rows in a field — usually around sixteen chicks to each hen. This was the worst job of all — giving the chicks to the hens. Firstly, you had to get her to settle down in her coop. Anyway, when this was accomplished and she was crouching you started to give her the chicks, pushing them in under her feathers until they were all out of sight, sheltered and warm against her body. After this you had to shut the front of the coop so that hen and chicks were left in darkness for a time. When about three hundred chicks had been placed with hens in this way you then patrolled back and fore listening for any signs of disturbance in the coops. If you heard cheeping coming from any of them you knew that chicks had got out from under the hen so you had to open the door and see to it that they went back again. Sometimes it took ages to get this done and you could only be satisfied that you'd done your job well when there was absolute silence in every coop. But some hens would never accept the pheasant chicks. Whenever they felt them under their bodies they would just rise up and kill them at once.

With rearing under way it meant working tremendously long hours — starting sometimes as early as four o'clock in the morning, there in the field all the time right through until darkness fell. There was a hut in the rearing field with all the equipment, food and water for the chicks and hens, and when things were really busy that hut was your home. The coops had to be opened every morning so that the little chicks could get out to run about and at night you had to shut them up after making sure they were all safely tucked up with their hens. And when you were doing this you had to creep about

207

the field as silently as you could. If you made a noise on the side of the coop, out the little blighters would rush, running all over the place. All the food had to be mixed and prepared thoroughly — hard-boiled eggs chopped up and shredded into meal. This took hours, sometimes, to get it right. But when the time came for the maturing chicks to be taken out and placed in coverts in the woods all the hard work you had done was well rewarded by the sight of them stalking about in the undergrowth in their new territory.

The big times in the shooting calendar on the estate are grouse shooting from August 12 onwards and the pheasant shoots, which — though they could start in October — usually happen in December when there's a good, crisp frost on the ground. There's quite an amount of work involved in planning a day's shooting, and with pheasants most of it is done in woodland. The guns are placed at strategic points at the edge of a wood or in a clearing and the beaters make their way through the wood rattling walking sticks against the trees, disturbing the undergrowth and bushes, so that the birds are forced up into the air to fly off and over the waiting guns. Some people have the mistaken idea that in some way it's cruel to rear pheasants so that they are, in their view, practically tame, then put them out in the woods to be shot. This is a fallacy. Once a reared pheasant has been out in the coverts for a week or so that bird is no different to a bird that has been hatched and reared in the wild. They are all wily, nervous birds and they act in this way whenever danger threatens. So they're off at the first hint of trouble and fly just as swiftly, just as confidently, as any other completely wild pheasant. Although the main purpose in raising young birds every year is for the shooting season, this has helped to maintain a substantial stock in the wild at all times of the year. In fact, in some places there are very few pheasants to be seen by anyone where no rearing is done. So it works both ways — there are birds to be shot and plenty who escape to establish a good stock in the wild.

In fact the same thing can be said for grouse. They're not reared, but the moorland is looked after in order to ensure that a breeding stock is maintained. In the spring, areas of heather are burned in controlled strips so that there will be plenty of fresh, green shoots available for the young birds later in the year. This is their staple diet. Now, if the heather were simply left alone it would become long and rank after a number of years. The grouse can't live among stuff like that. So they would fly away in search of more hospitable ground. I think it's worth making these points about both the pheasant and the grouse in order to show that there is something more to this business of gamekeeping other than simply making things easy for people to shoot these birds.

Being a gamekeeper is a very happy way of life. I don't say you'll ever get very rich at it, but the happiness is there and that counts for far more than money. Once you become a head gamekeeper you have lots of freedom. You're pretty well your own boss. Of course, it's a job where dedication to it is one of the prime essentials. Many of the younger men being taken on nowadays expect to be able to work the same hours as everyone else — a five-day week of forty hours or so. Well, of course, this is nonsense if standards are going to be maintained. To do the job properly demands an attitude of mind that realizes it is something you have to be involved in completely — for the full seven days of the week. Not working all the time, mind you, but appreciating that on any

209

day of the week you may find it necessary to do something in connection with the job. But then, on the other hand, this is where the freedom comes into it. Basically, you work your own hours and can have your own time off to suit yourself. But now, the new element in gamekeeping — at least some of them — expect the full freedom and think they should only work five days a week and have every weekend off. It can't be done. They don't seem to realize that they can't have the old-style freedom that goes with the job and the right to work a carefully controlled number of hours. And if gamekeeping is carried out to a strict timetable of hours — well, you're not going to have a very efficient or productive game department at the end of the day.

Today's gamekeeper is a different brand of gamekeeper altogether from the type of man who used to enter the job before the Second World War. In my case, my father, my grandfather, great-grandfather and great-great-grandfather had all been gamekeepers. And all the gamekeepers with whom I came in contact in my starting days in the late 1920s had been descended from a long line of gamekeepers. By the age of five I was fully capable of setting a trap to catch a hooded crow and able to bait and set a trap for a fox or a stoat. I knew how to snare rabbits and find a hooded crow's nest without having to go round every tree in the district. This entails you having to watch the face of a hill where you see them working and with experience you soon learn how to narrow the area where their nest might be to about forty square yards or so. The hooded crow is a pest of the first order. Nothing is safe from it — game birds, their eggs, their chicks, as well as many other birds, from chaffinches and robins up to plovers and lapwings. They are cunning devils and will do all they can —

a pair of them — to rob a nest of its eggs or chicks. I would say that any right-thinking gamekeeper sees red every time he hears one cawing or sees it flying overhead.

Anyhow, all these various tasks, essential to a gamekeeper's job, were therefore ingrained into me at a very early age. So, by the time I started doing the job properly and being paid for it I was, in effect, reasonably qualified. But nowadays ninety per cent of all gamekeepers who start off as young men straight from school, well, their fathers were probably miners or bricklayers or something just as totally different from what I would expect. That is why, as I mentioned earlier, unfortunately, gamekeeping has just become another job, rather than a distinct way of life. I'm not saying that some of these men never make good gamekeepers. A few of them do — the ones whose hearts are in the job. But there's another problem rarely encountered before — quite a lazy element has crept in and this is having harmful effects. I've already described how this job has freedom — how you are left on your own for much of the time (even as an under-keeper) to get on with it. Nobody need really know whether or not you're out on your beat on the estate doing what is required of you. I mean, there are parts of the estate where you as the gamekeeper may be the only man to set foot for months on end. So the opportunities are there for you to get away to some remote corner of the estate and just loaf around if that's the way your mind works. Well, as you can see, it is the greatest job on earth for "dodging the column"; whereas in days now sadly past dedication was the driving factor — the main force — in any gamekeeper's life. To go back to the subject of hooded crows — my own father would have been horrified if even as few as three of them were seen on his beat during the grouse-shooting season. But now — well, it's laughable sometimes; it's not uncommon for foxes to be seen running, as bold as brass, through the grouse drives when a shoot is on, as well as hooded crows flying around all over the place, even among the grouse as they sweep past over the butts. And all this ridiculous state of affairs has come about because a sense of pride has vanished, completely disappeared; this pride that once every gamekeeper had in him to see to it that the game was abundant and the vermin numbers as low as possible, is something you very rarely find now. And as a result the whole appearance of the estate is bound to suffer.

You see this situation all the time on some grouse moors. Up there the fox and the hooded crow are among the worst enemies you have. One fox can kill a tremendous number of birds in a year and there's nothing more expert than the hooded crow when it comes to robbing the nests of the grouse. If you find a tree where a hooded crow has a nest full of youngsters I guarantee it's quite possible you'll be able to count forty, fifty or even sixty grouse eggs — the shells — at the foot of that tree. And they're only the ones that have been brought back to the nest. So it's quite easy to see that if you have a gamekeeper who is not doing his job properly on a grouse moor then when it comes to the shooting season there are going to be precious few birds for anyone to shoot. And while this at one time might just have been an embarrassment to the laird, today it's fatal. You can't attract people to pay a high rent for grouse shooting if there are not enough birds around to make it worthwhile.

There is a great emphasis today on the conservation of various species of birds and animals, many of them highly

212

unpopular species in the eyes of most gamekeepers. But, in my opinion, I don't think the protection of some of these hawks and the like has made the slightest difference to either their numbers or the attitude of most gamekeepers towards them. Certainly, the modern gamekeeper is — or he should be — more aware of the true nature of some of the birds and animals regarded as his traditional enemies. For instance, many years ago it was common policy on the majority of estates to kill the otter. He was supposed to be harmful to salmon and a threat to the fishing. Sorry to say I did kill some in my young days. I didn't know any better at the time. But over the years I began to realize that the otter could actually benefit a good salmon river because he hunted for trout and eels, both enemies of the salmon parr. The number of mature salmon he ever took was negligible and then only in the depths of winter when, perhaps, sections of the river were frozen over and his food supply became limited. Once I realized this I refused to kill another otter and as far as I'm concerned everyone else should leave them alone. But if a gamekeeper has a grouse moor to protect he will do all in his power to see that the young grouse are safely hatched and looked after so that the guests or paying clients can have the best possible sport when the "Glorious Twelfth" comes around in August, and the shooting season begins.

As far as I am concerned I never gave the killing of any real predator a second thought when I was a young gamekeeper. It was something inbred and instilled into me as a youngster that the grouse had to be protected and that was the first and foremost thought in my mind as I went out on my beat. The fact that something I might be shooting — a particular species of hawk or whatever — might be what is now called "an endangered species" was something that never entered my head. Of course, the conservation movement is relatively new on the scene. People only started to think seriously about all this in the 1960s when it was found there were so few peregrine falcons and hobby hawks around. But up until then no one, except perhaps a mere handful of dedicated naturalists, ever bothered their heads about wildlife of any kind. No, it wasn't because we as gamekeepers were unthinking or totally ignorant when it came to us waging war on the predators on an estate. It was our job to do so. If we hadn't done it, or had done it badly, then we would have been bad gamekeepers and mark my words that was a state of affairs that would not have been tolerated in my young days. In a way the same reasoning is true for today. If we don't keep down the numbers of predators always lurking around on any estate we are, to a certain extent, failing in our jobs. So we still take a shot at them if we think it's necessary. We're more discriminating. And because of the state of public opinion about safeguarding wildlife in the present day we are, if we're wise, a great deal more careful in how we go about it.

Away back in the late twenties and thirties just keeping the Big House larders stocked with meat was quite a large part of the gamekeeper's job apart from the organized shoots. Meat was kept fresh and game — pheasants, grouse and woodcock — by putting it in the ice house down beside the gas plant which provided lighting throughout the house. Then there was the big cool larder with marble slabs and walls right beside the house itself. This was nearly as cold as the ice house. Roe deer and venison from the stags in the deer forest were kept hanging in both places and it was so cold, especially in the ice house, that meat would keep fresh for ages. The ice house was built into a bank with a door in front and on top there was a hatch. Periodically a load of ice would arrive and the hatch would be opened and the whole lot tipped inside. It was like having a gigantic deep-freeze outdoors. And the ice stayed solid for a long time. But it was no place in which no linger if you had to go in there for any reason. On a summer's day when you opened the door and went inside it was like stepping into the middle of winter. Within a minute or two the goose-pimples were out on your arms and your teeth were chattering.

At one time every estate of a reasonable size would have had its own blacksmith at work in a building known as the smiddy situated in the heart of the estate. Now, the permanent resident blacksmith no longer exists. He has been replaced either by an estate worker who does some other job for most of the week and who only spends a few hours on blacksmith's duties or, more often than not, by a travelling blacksmith who arrives in a van, just another port of call on his daily round.

At one time on this estate we had a big powerful chap as blacksmith. Most blacksmiths were, as I remember them, heavily built, strong individuals. They had to be, of course, because it was a job requiring not only a high degree of skill and precision, but much strength as well. This fellow was a young man and as big and powerful as any man. The Home Farm had six pairs of horses, Clydesdales; there were all the deer ponies used by the stalkers and quite an amount of work in connection with ponies and traps. So a great amount of his time was taken up in shoeing the horses and if he wasn't doing that he was making iron gates. There used to be iron gates all over the place on this estate — across the drives, on paths along the river banks. He could turn his hand to anything at all, could this fellow. He had only the bare necessities — the bellows, the fire and all the old-time blacksmith's essentials. He was a craftsman throughout. A typical village blacksmith, a big jovial type. He did all the metal work for carts for the farms and the forestry department, plough shares which were often broken because of the stony ground. It was a full-time job. Now and again when he would be inundated with work he'd be given assistance from one of the estate workers, someone from the general labouring gang.

His forge always smelt of burning hooves. The furnace would be going full blast, sending out a fierce heat which, in the summer, made you sweat whenever you set foot in the place. And there was this smell, quite a pleasant smell really — highly aromatic. There was a continuous clatter of metal on to metal, plenty of dirt of course, cobwebs, horse shoes hanging all over the place in the various sizes he would have shaped ready for the finishing touch. He would do that in his spare time. Also, great racks of iron, all thicknesses and lengths.

But gradually, especially from the mid-1950s onwards, the work started to dry up. It got less and less as farms became fully mechanized and needed the services, not of a blacksmith, but a fully qualified engineer who knew about the engines of the new machines as well as their mechanical parts. Some blacksmiths adapted and were able to cope to quite a large extent, but for the full-time estate blacksmith, well, his days were numbered. When he retired he was not replaced and what work was still available was contracted out. Now, the travelling blacksmith arrives on the appointed

216

day. He has a large van carrying all his equipment, portable forge heated by gas cylinders. There's nothing romantic about it now. It's the most practical way of doing the job.

As a gamekeeper who has been around this estate for a very long time, one of the things I miss most of all is the absence of the big social occasions of the past. In my young days there was always a dance to go to. Nearly every night around the festive season the estate employees would be invited to parties and dances. There were also often weddings at this time of the year because people had holidays and were able to have the time off to get married. One wedding which I remember well took place on New Year's Eve — Hogmanay. The bride was a farmer's daughter and the groom the assistant head forester.

The church was beautifully decorated with flowers from many of the estate workers' gardens and as they stood in front of the minister bride and groom made a splendid couple, although the best man had decided for some reason or other to shave off his long moustache and looked distinctly odd as a result. With the ceremony over everyone then went to the farm house where we had drinks and a piece of wedding cake. Here, a lot of handshaking took place as the guests wished the young couple health and prosperity. After an hour or so the minister and the farmer's wife led the way to the granary in one of the main farm buildings where the feast and wedding dance were to take place. Everyone had to pick a partner so I saw one of the daughters of another neighbouring farmer sitting by herself and asked her to accompany me. She did.

The granary, up a flight of stairs on the outside of the building, was lit by hurricane lamps suspended from the beams and decorated with flowers and bracken and all sorts of greenery from coniferous trees — all this work done by the gardeners on the estate. It was a huge, high building, almost two hundred feet long with tables set from end to end and laden with every sort of food — hams and cuts of beef, cakes and scones, puddings. At regular intervals stood decanters with whisky and wine, the whole feast laid out on gleaming white table cloths. At the far end was a raised platform with a piano standing at one side.

Once we were all seated, and by now those who had been at the church service and in the farm house had been joined by dozens of others, the minister said grace. Then the feast began, the granary filled with the sound of voices, talking and laughing, the clatter of forks and knives and the clinking of cups and glasses. When everyone had eaten as much as possible — and for some of us young unmarried chaps it was the chance to taste any number of things we didn't ever get in the normal run of events — there were the usual speeches and toasts. With these over, the high point of the evening arrived — the dance. Most of the young men lent a hand to clear away the majority of the tables although some were left at one side in a corner with glasses and drink and cuts of ham, ready for people to help themselves as they wished.

The dancing got under way with the Grand March, once again the minister and the farmer's wife taking the lead by being first on the floor. For music we had the piano, two fiddles and a cornet. There was also a piper for the reels. I played the fiddle so joined in and played for the first few dances. This was a job that I often had to do at our estate dances and it gave me great enjoyment. All the same it did keep me from lots of fun and exploits — pure mischief, of

218

course — and there were times when I regretted being a bit of a musician. However, my brother was present at the dance and as he was a very good fiddler I asked him to help out too, so that I could take part in the festivities.

The granary was looking magnificent, brightly decorated, the lamps glowing, the dancers enjoying themselves, faces flushed in the heat, and the others — men and women — having a drink while they watched the proceedings. Around the walls were benches and chairs and on these sat a large number of old folk, because almost without exception every person among the workers and tenants on the estate was there for the wedding dance. When I was young I always had a good laugh at the old-timers sitting watching us young folks having a good time. The men would be complaining, no doubt, about the way the dancing had changed for the worse since their own young days and the women would find plenty to gossip about by having a go at the clothes worn by the girls and how, when they had been young themselves, they'd never have worn frocks like that or held on to their partners in this new free and easy way. I expect I'd do the same thing, now that I'm one of the old ones myself, but there are few real country dances nowadays where it's a case of the whole community getting together. That was one of the really good things about the past: all ages mingled at social occasions in the countryside and on an estate where everyone knew everyone else; it was, in a way, always like a great big family get-together. Anyhow, there we were inside the granary, snug and warm with the fiddles and piano going for all they were worth and the dancers pounding the floor. None of us had a care for the storm outside because, it being the middle of winter, there were always gales and frost — more often than not several feet of snow falling practically every other night.

I had a dance with the bride — the Lancers — and tried to get some information about where she was going on her honeymoon. But, true to form, she was not telling and with a laugh and a smile dodged answering when I tried to trick her into making some sort of hint. When, later that evening the hired car arrived to take the couple away the bagpipes played and we fastened bundles of old shoes to the car's back bumper and showered them with confetti to give them the traditional send off.

As the dance went on none of us took any notice of the time. Long past midnight the granary was the happiest place on the whole estate and, judging by the crowd, the place where everyone had gathered. We toasted each other at midnight to celebrate the start of another year and were prepared to dance the night away in honour of this and the marriage that had just taken place. Everybody, old and young, was having the time of their lives, the young ones dancing without a break and the old folks gossiping and joking among themselves. One group of four old men, local worthies as we called them, sat in a corner near the band and each one of them was smoking a pipe filled with black twist tobacco.

There was so much smoke pouring up from them it was hard to see any of them sometimes or, when I was playing myself, to see what the dancers were doing on the floor.

Around half past two in the morning myself and Jimmie, one of my pals and an estate gardener, were both asked by the farmer to fetch some more whisky and refreshments from the farm house. He gave me the keys to a scullery and with hurricane lamps we went down the steps of the granary and across the yard. It was a bitterly cold night, clear and frosty, with a chilling north-easterly wind blowing down from the moor. Some snow had fallen and there were footprints frozen into shape to mark the departure of some folk who had decided to go home earlier. In the scullery we found a ten-gallon jar of proof whisky, plenty of wine and soft drinks. There were two copper kettles hanging from hooks on a shelf. The farmer had given us strict instructions not to be sparing with this next consignment of whisky so I said to Jimmie, "You fill one of those kettles out of the whisky jar and I'll take a syphon of soda and the other kettle full of water."

When we returned to the granary we went round everybody, filling up their glasses, but not one of them would touch the soda water. They all informed me that they preferred proper water in their whisky, if, indeed, they were going to mix it with anything at all. By this time even some of the older folks, who had just been sitting about all night, were showing signs of becoming properly merry so this gave me the idea of playing a trick on them.

It wasn't all that long before we had to go back to the farm house for fresh supplies and this time we filled both kettles full to the brim with whisky and never bothered about water. Jimmie said to me, "I bet we'll soon have the old folks up dancing once they get this lot inside them." So, off we went again, across the yard and up the steps, the noise of the laughter and voices and the music quite loud even in the open air. It was really hot inside the granary and a real pleasure to get inside again after the biting wind sweeping across the farm. Round the granary we went dispensing our whisky to men and women alike. Jimmie went first and I came behind offering water to all who wanted it. By now, most folk just said to me, "Fill her up," then pushed their glass in my direction. So I just did this — did what I was asked to do; except that instead of the water they were expecting I topped up their glasses with more whisky. One or two did remark that it tasted very strong and asked for some more water. So I obliged. And no one suspected a thing because they'd already had quite a bit to drink, the farmer being well known both for his generosity and for favouring a good, strong whisky.

The effects of my "dope" became obvious within about twenty minutes. Heads began to shake and a good number of old cronies rose unsteadily from their seats and said they must be going home. A few couldn't even make it to the door and had to be led out and down the steps where, in the yard, they tottered about, each trying to help the other to get his or her bearings in order to find the road leading away from the farm. Practically everyone was on foot, although a few had come to the dance on bicycles and it was quite a sight to see them all stumbling away. Then, with them gone, we went on dancing for another couple of hours and at five o'clock in the morning decided to finish and go home ourselves.

What a glorious night it had been. And you know, the great thing about it was that it wasn't just an isolated event. The wedding feast was special, of course, but many dances of this kind were held then on the estate in one farm or another. The laird put up most of the money for the building of a hall later on and the dances went on there as well as lots of other events. There was plenty of fun and plenty of laughter and I think we all worked the harder as a result. Certainly, this type of social occasion

222

made us all very much a proper community. And that's something you'd find it hard to say today about any estate. For most, an estate has just become a place of work.

There are very few occasions now when the laird and his family get together with their tenants and employees for a social occasion, but when I was young it was a regular occurrence every year. And everybody loved it. There was always some sort of function at Christmas and the New Year, but the main highlight was the ball at the start of the grouse-shooting season when a large shooting party was resident in the Big House. Everyone attended — the shooting guests, tenants, employees and, to the delight of the younger men, quite a number of English girls up from the south to help cope with all the additional work in the house.

The estate's recreation hall was used for this and it had a lovely dance floor. The gardeners decorated the walls and ceiling with flowers cut from the magnificent herbaceous borders and great sprays of heather in full bloom brought down from the moor. A few days before the ball was due to take place, usually around August 25, the gamekeepers were detailed by the laird to teach all the English girls how to do the steps of the Scottish country dances. He was very keen on dancing himself and looked forward to the event with as much enthusiasm as we did. On the morning of the ball the final touches were made to the hall and the floor. Made of pitchpine and polished to magnificence, the surface was so slippery that some of the farmers — and others — who attended without proper dancing shoes were hardly able to stop themselves from falling over.

Dancing began at 11 p.m. The music was provided by a well-known band hired from one of the larger towns and the laird was first to lead off in the Grand March. At times there could be around one hundred and twenty couples on the floor and in my mind as I think back I can still hear the music and see the splendid sight of the house gentlemen in full Highland dress, kilts and brilliant jackets, buckles and buttons gleaming, every colour of tartan — and the ladies, every one of them with a tartan sash across the front of their evening gowns. They also had long trains attached to their dresses and these they very cleverly looped on their arm. All us gamekeepers were in Highland dress too, and although the kilt was paid for by the laird, because he required us to wear it while out shooting, the jackets, hose and dancing shoes were bought by ourselves.

At midnight supper was served in a large hall in the Big House itself — hams, cold meat, game and every kind of pudding, trifles, custard, the lot. There were so many guests at the ball that everyone had to go to the supper in relays — thirty or forty couples at a time. The dancing was great fun, plenty of traditional Scottish dances — eightsome reels, strathspeys and the like, with the laird making sure that all his gamekeepers partnered the most distinguished of his lady guests. This was, of course, quite a good thing to do because it made things a lot better when we were all out shooting on the moor; it made for a much friendlier atmosphere all round. Although I say it myself I was quite a good dancer and enjoyed it very much. I'd had some lessons, which helped me a great deal. The only thing that worried me was having to cope with the long trains on their dresses, but somehow or other I managed to avoid any nasty accidents. This was more than could be said for some of my companions, a few of them being fairly clumsy on their feet at the best of times. They became entangled in the trains, to the embarrassment of both the ladies and themselves and I'm sure some of the ladies must have had harsh words to say about their host, the laird, for insisting that such rough individuals had to dance with them from time to time throughout the night.

Around one o'clock in the morning it was the usual practice for the people from the Big House to depart, after a speech of thanks had been made by one of the laird's tenants. But within half an hour or so some of the younger ones would be back to rejoin the fun, which always carried on until between four and five o'clock.

On one occasion after a summer ball I was making my way back to the bothy clutching a leg of roast mutton which had been given to me by one of the footmen in the Big House. It was broad daylight and I was on a path going through a wood. All of a sudden I heard a voice alongside of me and out of the bushes stepped the laird. For a moment I just stood there in front of him, holding the leg of mutton by the shank bone. I didn't even have time to throw it away and although I got on well with him I wasn't sure if he'd take too kindly to my smuggling home a sizeable roast no doubt intended for his own table. But he gave a great grin when he saw it as well as the uncomfortable expression on my face. He said that instead of going off to bed after he had left the ball he had taken a rifle and gone roe deer stalking. He had managed to shoot three beasts and wanted me to bring them in to prepare them for placing in the larder. "After you've had a sleep, of course," he said. Then, with a laugh, pointing to the leg of mutton, "and when you've had a bite to eat."

225

Fortunately, this estate still places quite an emphasis on the sporting side although, as I've said, the bulk of the shooting and fishing is purely commercial now. The estates run on the old sporting system are by far the best ones to work on. If you can get a job on one of those you've got the best of all possible worlds. You've got your entertainment laid on, invariably you're supplied with your own transport and you can have the freedom of the wide open spaces as well. It's good to know there are still a few estates where a gamekeeper is still a gamekeeper, and a gardener, though he may be the only one, is still a gardener. But on so many places now they are incorporating jobs so that you get a gamekeeper/shepherd; gamekeeper/cattleman; gamekeeper/handyman. Take the forestry department. Well, you can be switched to any job there. There's not much chance now on most estates of going there as a pure forester, gamekeeper, shepherd or gardener. You are liable to be thrown in at the deep end and expected to do other jobs. It's only the wealthier estates or the big sporting estates which are making money from the sporting side, salmon fishing, grouse and pheasant shooting, deer stalking, where a man can be really true to his trade.

It wouldn't suit me to have to do another job linked to being a gamekeeper. At least I'm fortunate here. But then, so often, life is what you make it for yourself. I suppose if I were a younger man I would adapt and accept the new ways. I suppose I'd have to if I wanted to go on working out of doors. You can put up with a lot when you have a job in such magnificent surroundings; where, even when it rains, you find you're not really bothered. What's the point of complaining when, as far as I'm concerned, estate life of any sort is still a far better existence than working for a living in some grimy town. There might be more money to be made in a town, but there's precious little fresh air — or freedom. I put a high value on being able to enjoy both.

CHAPTER
FIFTEEN

Maxwell Johnstone is a laird with a particularly business-like approach to the traditional role he has to play as the owner of Strathalder estate. He sees no other way for its continued existence than to follow the now conventional commercial path, exploiting the resources inherited from his father in order to ensure economic survival both for the estate as a meaningful place and for the people he employs. As a result he has few illusions about his position as laird.

Although the property has been in his family's hands for over a century he freely admits to the burden of being expected to behave as some of his more wealthy ancestors did, when, in reality, his personal financial position and circumstances allow for no more than a shadow of the once luxurious lifestyle enjoyed by his predecessors. Like so many lairds of the present day he has substantial business interests outside his estate. He could exist quite independently without it. But, just as the tradition of working on an estate has been bred into many of the men he now employs so, too, does he feel the need to fulfil an obligation that has come his way as a result of ancestry. It is a matter from which the element of choice has been removed. Birth saw to it that he became the guardian of a legacy from the past.

I inherited the estate shortly after the Second World War, when my father died. I was thirty-one then and well aware of the tremendous responsibilities that had been placed on my shoulders. Of course, I had helped my father from time to time with estate business, but despite my attempts to be realistic about the problems, never envisaged for a moment that in future years life would be so fraught with difficulties.

Now, I suppose to the majority of people who live on the estate, I am seen as, and considered to be, a very wealthy man. Compared with the average working man I expect that I am. But it's relative. Certainly, I have a fine house — to me a most beautiful house — with large gardens and privacy, thousands of acres of land, salmon fishing, deer stalking, grouse shooting, all manner of leisurely pursuits at my elbow whenever I wish to take them up. These things would be on the credit side. But what most people fail to appreciate, completely fail to see, are the drawbacks to being an estate owner, the sort of thing that in my father's day would never have been given a second thought because, quite frankly, money was no object then. My father was the archetypal laird. He lived permanently on the estate, apart from a month or two in London each year; he visited estate workers' homes and tried to be of some help when any family was in difficulties of one kind or another; he entertained his guests on a lavish scale and was just as considerate towards his tenants and employees at Christmas and the New Year, with parties and dances here in the mansion house. When he wanted a new house built for an employee he just issued the necessary instructions to his factor, who put the job in hand, and when tenant farmers came seeking repairs and improvements to their land and buildings while, perhaps, he did not always consider such requests with a sympathetic ear, at least if he did he could agree to the schemes without a twinge as regards the money he would have to pay out. What a truly splendid way in which to order one's life and affairs.

Today, I find myself forced to operate an estate on a very strict budget and when it comes to improvements and repairs have always to think twice and ask myself is this or that proposal absolutely necessary? This situation has arisen due to a variety of circumstances which started with my father's death and the amount of death duties which were levied at the time. The sum we had to find was simply enormous, even by the standards of the late 1940s, and in order to pay it and finalize matters once and for all, I had to sell a small portion of the estate. Fortunately, my neighbour wanted some more river so it was a fairly simple matter to put the deal through. I sold him a length of the opposite bank and this in no way harmed the overall pattern of the estate. In reality it remained very much as it had always been. Nowadays, of course, with capital gains tax and the prospect of a wealth tax being imposed always looming on the horizon, God knows what sort of financial debacle will confront my son when I pass on. I've taken steps to alleviate the problems for him in the future by taking advantage of all the legitimate means at my disposal, but it's a hard job to keep pace with bureaucracy today and no longer possible to play the game according to the rules. The trouble is — they keep changing the rules whenever it suits them.

All this, of course, purely concerns the future. What worries me most is the present. As laird and the employer of a fairly large work force I am confronted continually with all manner of obstacles which, nowadays, the State manages to strew in the path of business men. There are now so many rules and regulations concerning employees that, quite frankly, one is forced to the conclusion that the odds are heavily weighted against the employer and stacked very much in favour of the worker. Don't misunderstand me on this subject. I am no tyrant when it comes to what I expect from those I employ. Quite simply, all I require of anyone in estate employment is a reasonable effort to the best of his or her ability in return for the not inconsiderable wages now being paid. I fully realize and appreciate that measures had to be introduced and steps taken to safeguard working people and give them some additional security, redundancy payments, protection against unfair dismissal, a variety of things of this nature. To a degree I approved of the social justice of such measures in much the same way as those introduced by Parliament in the sphere of property letting. But just as this has now gone hopelessly wrong, with the result that it's now the landlords who are having to seek some form of protection against tenants (mainly, by refusing to let property) so, too, does an employer find that he has no room for manoeuvre once he has engaged someone to work for him. It's rather like a case of "Till death us do part" now, whether or not the employee proves good at his job or is a complete and utter failure.

Now, while this may be a bad enough situation for an industrial employer running a factory, the position is worse, in my opinion, on an estate. The work force must operate as part of a team so it only takes one awkward customer to cause problems and resentment among the rest. And what can I do? Absolutely nothing, just so long as he does the bare minimum and is not criminally negligent in the performance of his duties. Yes, there are occasions when I long for the authority wielded by my father as laird. He was always fair, mind you, but when circumstances warranted a firm hand then he wasted no opportunity in confronting the problem. My difficult and lazy employee would have been given his marching orders had he been around in my father's day. And any right-thinking person would surely agree that such a character deserved dismissal. Now, as I say, I'm stuck with him and if I do try to get rid of him I have to ensure that I'm not being unfair or unreasonable, plus any number of other equally irritating qualifications. It doesn't seem to matter how unreasonable the difficult worker is; he seems to be able to do whatever he pleases and I'm the one who has to suffer.

It is of prime importance that I get the maximum return from every possible aspect of the estate. Every resource to hand must be exploited. It sounds a terribly mercenary attitude but, believe me, it is the only recipe for survival. Let me be quite frank and blunt about that. And it's worth bearing in mind that if, for any reason, I go under financially it will not only be myself and my family who suffer, but every single one of the people who work on the estate. They are dependent on it — on me — for work. Some of them have always worked on this estate, their fathers before them. Their lives are totally bound up with the place. To them it is their home. And I have no wish to endanger this security they feel — this sense of oneness they have for their particular slice of the world. They have just as much right to be a part of it as I have. It's something I always try hard to remember.

In many cases the only possible way to sell an estate of this kind — a general estate encompassing forestry, agriculture, game shooting, deer stalking and salmon fishing — is to divide it into separate units and try to obtain the best possible price for each segment. Deer stalking and salmon fishing are reasonably easy to find buyers for at the moment, even game shooting, and agricultural land always finds a ready market; but when it comes to forestry, if the commercial timber is still young, then it's purely a long-term investment. Of course one might find a rich Arab gentleman who would welcome the chance of acquiring the estate as it stands — everything — but as a rule that would be one's only hope of keeping the place intact and still realizing the best possible price. I mean to say the total value of this estate runs into several million pounds and where in Britain today will you find anyone with that sort of money willing to spend it on a venture of this nature? It would be rather like searching for the proverbial needle in the haystack.

It would hurt me very much if I was ever forced to sell. More so, if I had to split up the estate in order to do it. It has been in the family since 1867 — there are well over a hundred years of tradition to think of, not only regarding my own family, but with some of the employees too. This is what I find fascinating when I consider it. The laird and worker have been bound together in this fashion for so long. It's like a marriage. Continuity is the keyword. I have no desire to do anything that might hinder or damage this unique state of affairs. That's why I have to be absolutely ruthless in pruning costs to the bone and developing any part of the estate which is able to produce income. My father and his father before him could run the estate purely from their own pockets. I cannot do this.

I don't resent what might be termed an intrusion on my privacy by having had to offer my moorland and river for letting. Why should I? Many of the people who come here to go deer stalking or fish for salmon have become friends. But generally speaking I don't see a great deal of them. I am usually too busy and away from here for part of each week attending to other business interests. Management of the estate is in the hands of my factor. A good factor is a great asset to any estate owner. He is the laird's right-hand man. He should be the sort of chap who can advise on every aspect of the business and be able to formulate policy with you in order to achieve the smooth running of the estate. Some lairds whom I know, in particular a few of the younger ones, have dispensed with the services of factors. They prefer to do the job themselves. Some are quite good as it. Others are not. What many of them do not realize is that if they are constantly involved in every single detail of estate management — the day-to-day mixture of trivia and matters of importance — they are in great danger of losing a sense of perspective when it comes to having to make a really major decision. Also, no matter how much a laird tries to soften them or break them down altogether, barriers do exist between many estate workers and their employer. Too much of an attempt to be in on every single thing is sometimes regarded by workers as interference. I know, it sounds stupid; but that's the way many of them feel when the owner or one of the family decides to lend a hand with, say, some forestry work; or when the laird is continually turning up to check on how a particular piece of work is proceeding. That's why I always work in conjunction with my factor. He reports to me, discusses any problems and plans. I take the final decisions. If there are any complaints then whoever may feel aggrieved can always come to see me — or I will go to see them — and an attempt can be made to resolve the issue. I can do this; act as the final judge. Everyone here knows it is my system of management. The laird who will not delegate authority does not enjoy the same freedom. He can never be regarded by his employees as completely impartial. As it happens, the way I prefer to work is exactly how my father handled estate business. So, in one respect at least, things haven't changed. The objectives may be different now, but the methods of achieving them and ensuring as much harmony as possible among employees and tenants remain the same.

The rural districts of this region of Scotland are, quite simply, held together by the existence of estates. Villages have been placed on the map as a result of having been built to house employees on an estate; whole communities owe their existence, their very life, to being in close proximity to an estate. In a way, country estates over the centuries have developed a pattern for the rural areas, not only by means of the general shape of things, but in the social fabric of the communities. Many country districts would have no community hall if it had not been for the generosity of some laird in past years. Going even further back in time, quite a few places would have been without schools, or indeed were without schools, until the laird financed the building of them. Also, here and there shops have been established through the laird seeing the need for such an enterprise and making available at low interest the capital needed by the right sort of person willing to start up such a business. Churches, too, have benefited from patronage and in our own community many repair bills for work done to the church building and the manse were paid by my father in his time. I'm afraid I don't do this myself, although I do try to help when I can, should there be any sort of crisis. So, a great number of people, directly and indirectly, have cause to be grateful for the structure and the system that brought and sustained a network of estates throughout the country.

No one ever likes to think of himself as a bad laird, I expect. Certainly, I hope no employee or tenant of mine regards me in this fashion. Oh yes, there are some black sheep around, but tell me of any walk of life where there are not? I'm sure many people still believe, misguidedly, that estates are an anachronism now; that it's wrong to have one man owning so much and wielding what appears to be a feudalistic form of power over those who live and work on his land. This reasoning, if it deserves such a description, always strikes me as a huge joke. Nothing could be further from the truth. And the people who utter such views, among them certain Members of Parliament who ought to know better, I suppose, are only instrumental in fomenting trouble where, in reality, none exists. I certainly don't feel feudal in any way whatsoever. Even in the different days of the past when my father was laird in the 1920s and 1930s I'm fairly certain he never behaved in a condescending or patronizing fashion towards tenants and employees.

I know this point of view may sound predictable and glib, but, truly, it's not meant to be. The only way — the best way — I can sum up the relationship between laird and employees on an estate is that it is like one huge family. I pride myself in attempting to maintain the harmony and balance of a large family. For most of the time I succeed, not because of any great skill on my part, but thanks to having a good factor and heads of department who know their jobs and see to it that complaints and grievances are dealt with instantly and not allowed to simmer into rank discontent. I try to keep myself up to date with matters affecting my employees — such developments as when there is going to be an addition to one of the families, the marriage of one of the single workers, a bereavement. I pay visits from time to time to the houses of the more senior employees. They seem to find this worthwhile. I know I certainly do and I gain a great deal from this more social contact. I don't go around the estate at Christmas and the New Year wishing everyone the compliments of the season (as my father did), but I do try to convey my best wishes to those who live and work on the estate through the various departmental heads. Yes, to be frank I like to know what is going on. This is not an attempt on my part to interfere with workers' and tenants' private lives, nor is it an exercise in man management — following text book principles to ensure the willing obedience of all on the pay roll.

Certainly not. I do these things because I honestly believe that, traditionally, I still have a role to play in acting responsibly towards those living and working on the estate. Any true laird in the past would have felt this way. I know my own father did. I see no reason for changing, even although I am now forced by circumstances beyond my control to run the estate as one would operate any modern business. I may need to make some sort of profit each year from all the various estate enterprises, but this need for financial viability

237

will never be allowed, if humanly possible, to overrule the most important consideration of the position I am privileged to enjoy — the maintenance of a pleasant and worthwhile environment for those people who, like me, regard this place as their home.

The north-east of Scotland and the Highlands are undergoing a transformation now due to the discovery of oil and gas in the North Sea. For the first time ever this region of the country finds itself in the middle of an expanding industrial economy when, traditionally, the main sources of revenue have been from agriculture and fishing and, of course, the distilling of whisky. Fishing is on the decline for a variety of reasons, whisky distilling maintains a steady and gradual expansion while agriculture, of course, will always be a major feature in the lives of people in this part of the world. Naturally, estates and agriculture go hand in hand. Many of the largest farms are now owned by estates. In my father's day the majority of estate farms were tenanted, but with changes to the tenancy laws and the increasing value of agricultural land it has now become common practice for estates to run the farms. When leases have expired I have always taken over the farms. There are still several farms in the hands of tenants, but despite increases in rents over recent years it's practically impossible for a modern estate to get very far by relying on the income from these. My policy on agriculture is to have the various farms individually responsible for one particular aspect. Several are almost completely arable farms for the growing of crops such as oats, potatoes, turnips and the like, one close to the moor looks after the sheep, another has a large pig unit, a couple concentrate on the fattening of beef cattle, while one has a dairy herd. As a result most aspects of the agricultural spectrum are handled and by giving each farm a particular role and allowing it to concentrate intensively on this I have been able to secure maximum productivity and profit even during the most difficult periods.

Getting people to work on the land — good, responsible people, that is — is becoming increasingly difficult, despite this being a traditional agricultural region where many generations of the same family have always worked on farms, very often in the same places. There are many reasons for this state of affairs. One new development has been the lure of the oil companies and many young men who otherwise would have become agricultural workers are now earning good money working for construction companies affiliated to the oil business. On this score agriculture or, indeed, general estate work can never compete with regard to wages. There will always be a large gap simply because large industrial concerns have the resources and we have not. I'm not saying that in general terms agricultural workers could not, or should not be paid more, but there really is a limit as to how far this can go at any particular time.

If I have a good year financially, then I'm only too willing to meet a wage claim because I can afford to do it; and, of course, my men have helped to ensure this additional prosperity. But if things haven't been going well, then I can only sustain a lack of profit for a limited time. Yet, despite this, I am still faced with the ever-increasing wage claim. I do pay key workers above the minimum scale, but conscientious and hardworking as many of them are, they never seem to realize and appreciate that there can be no more money for them if the estate, as a whole, hasn't succeeded in making money. Not that I am ever faced with any real trouble — quite honestly, country people are too level-headed for that. And, of course, the basic wage rates are agreed nationally. But it spoils the atmosphere when there has to be grumbling and a little bickering by either side. I know it's hard for many working people to make ends meet as a result of recent inflation. I know that in many instances the wives have to pay slightly higher prices for goods just because they happen to live in the heart of the countryside. I know that men will go elsewhere to work if they feel aggrieved and are unable to adequately maintain their families on what I pay them.

But every argument they put forward I can match with one of my own. I may be the laird but, in reality, I'm no different from any of them. Inflation has left its mark on me, as well — and on the estate. It is no respecter of persons. Take maintenance costs — buildings, fences, drives, hill roads; they have risen out of all proportion. A simple repair to a roof, say, which might have cost in the early 1970s something in the region of £100, is now nearer £700; a stretch of driveway requiring resurfacing — a few years ago, £1000; now, between £6000 and £7000. Well, I can't go on being able to afford all of these quite necessary and legitimate expenses if my business is not making a substantial return. Happily, things are going relatively well since I diversified into letting first salmon fishing and then deer stalking. The fishing is let on a weekly or fortnightly basis and the stalking by the week. I am also now reaping the benefits of tree planting schemes put into effect by my father when I was only a youngster. He was far ahead of his time initiating what are now termed re-afforestation schemes, planting extensively on barren moorland. I think quite a few of his neighbours, and I'm sure

240

even more of his employees, thought he was a trifle eccentric, to say the least, in putting trees into such areas of the estate. But he was right. Absolutely right. It is now a modern practice of forestry and thanks to his initiative and foresight this estate now has an abundance of fine, standing timber which in the past year or two I have started to fell and extract.

This is a perfect example of how much running an estate differs from the operation of any other business. One is constantly thinking far ahead, sometimes a long way beyond one's own lifetime. It is important to think not just in terms of one's own economic survival, but of that of one's children. As far as I am concerned, being now in my early sixties, the forestry schemes which I am putting into operation at the present time with the planting of young trees will be something my son will benefit from when the appropriate time comes. So often when arriving at decisions I have to bear in mind the long-term effect of my actions. And so much of what an estate depends on for revenue relies to a great extent on the forces of Nature. Despite all the twentieth-century technology available to mankind, Nature up here on a Scottish estate is Nature pure and simple, able to dictate its own terms when the mood so takes it.

For a number of years in the mid- and late-sixties this river, in common with most Scottish rivers, was plagued by a disease which affected the salmon. It was a particularly nasty and virulent disease — a form of white fungus which grew on the bodies of salmon, slowly killing them in much the same way that myxomatosis deals with the rabbit population. At certain times of the year hundreds of salmon, infected in varying degrees, were in the pools and it was no pleasure to fish when the evidence of so much disease was plain to see.

There was absolutely nothing we could do about it, beyond remove as many as possible from the river. Sometimes they had to be shot with rifles because there was simply no other way of getting them out of the water. It was a ghastly business and, of course, adversely affected the prospects of letting the river to interested anglers. As with most things in Nature, however, it gradually sorted itself out in its own way — and time — and things are now back to normal. But when it was at its peak, and there seemed to be no end in sight, it was a very worrying time.

Although I'm fully aware of the necessity to make every penny I can from the resources of the estate, I simply refuse to have caravan sites on the place. On several estates — some quite close to here — this has been done and there are not many which I don't consider to be an eyesore. I'm sure it would be lucrative because the tourist industry is booming in Scotland at the moment, but, frankly, I'd rather do without them. But some neighbouring lairds have gone into the holiday cottage and chalet business and made a success of it. So this I might try. After all, it would be a way of making it worthwhile to renovate and modernize some of the more remote and now uninhabited houses around the estate — the ones which for a variety of reasons one finds difficult to sell. It's possible to recoup one's costs from this sort of venture in a relatively short space of time, what with there being so many visitors to Scotland, not only in the summer, but during the winter months for ski-ing holidays and so forth. In addition to putting these properties into good shape again and enjoying the income from letting them, one would be adding to one's overall investment because of having made them habitable again. If they ever had to be sold, then it would be much easier to get rid of them as sound properties than as they stand at the moment.

It's hard to envisage that many estates could become much smaller and still remain as proper estates. A great many of the big ones have now been broken up into smaller units, just as was done here so long ago in Victorian times. In a way I was fortunate to inherit an estate of a manageable size, unlike some of my acquaintances who were faced with having to sell a major part of their land in order to meet death duties in recent years.

The future is uncertain, but then, on the other hand, this is what makes life interesting from my point of view. When I became laird here I accepted a challenge. Running a country estate in modern times is always a challenge. I have distinct responsibilities to my family, to myself and to the people who work here, to continue ensuring a healthy degree of prosperity for the estate. I must make it work. I've every indication that

my son, who will inherit from me, feels the same way. So, hopefully, the estate will continue to exist — and thrive, I hope — as it has always done, because in order to maintain our family pride we must accept our responsibilities as custodians of a part of the country's heritage.

Also available in ISIS Large Print:

Out with Romany

G. Bramwell Evens

"There are many ways of seeing the countryside. You can travel about in a car, you can pedal along on a bicycle, or you can use Shanks's pony. All of them have certain advantages, but if you have a caravan, you carry your home about with you."

This book deals with the intimate lives of the squirrel, fox and hedgehog in story form, and yet is full of information as to the life and habits of each animal. Romany, travelling about in his caravan, with his spaniel dog Raq, introduces these wild animals to Tim, the farmer's small son, and, whilst watching them, throws fascinating sidelights on the ways of the snipe, curlew, owl, rabbit, stoat, kestrel and other wild creatures.

ISBN 978-0-7531-5691-9 (hb)
ISBN 978-0-7531-5692-6 (pb)

Goodbye, Wigan Pier

Ted Dakin

"My escape from a school that taught me very little was a euphoric occasion and because of the headmaster's ruling that only short pants should be worn by all pupils, my first pair of long ones was an added bonus."

Ted Dakin returns to his childhood in Wigan, with more stories of the people and places he grew up with. He tells of boxing matches ruled over by his vindictive headmaster, Owd Hector Wainwright; of men stealing coal from the trains; and of his first job in a saddlery. Full of the characters of his youth, like Dolly Varden and her predictions, Fag-Ash Lil and Dunkirk veteran Ginger Dyson, Ted's stories are full of the warmth and wit of a Wigan lad.

ISBN 978-0-7531-9510-9 (hb)
ISBN 978-0-7531-9511-6 (pb)

A Garden in the Hills

Katharine Stewart

"I stretch up, easing those back muscles, then hunker down again, nose nearer to the weeding. There's quite a comfort about this position, all one's person in close contact with the earth."

Katharine Stewart lived, for many years, in an old school house with a large garden in the beautiful wild country near Loch Ness. This is a celebration of gardening, one of mankind's oldest pleasures. Month by month we are taken through a year in the life of Katharine's garden. The circle of the seasons is luminously evoked as we are told of the practicalities of gardening, cooking, bee-keeping and wine-making. Katharine's writing is full of warm, personal insights, good humour and a love of living things. The joy of nature extends from her garden into all aspects of life.

ISBN 978-0-7531-9504-8 (hb)
ISBN 978-0-7531-9505-5 (pb)

Rathcormick

Homan Potterton

"By some quirk or other, I was different in temperament to my brothers so that despite being the youngest of a very large and happy family, I frequently felt that I was an oddity, an outsider."

Rathcormick is the name of the substantial farmhouse in County Meath that was unexpectedly left to Homan's parents on the condition that they provided a male heir. They provided two daughters and six sons for good measure!

Homan's memoir is a sensitive, often bittersweet, depiction of a marriage, of the pains and joys of childhood and of life in rural Ireland in the 1950s. For Homan, the youngest of the eight children, life was a free-spirited awakening in an adult world of old-fashioned virtue and frugality. He recalls the moment that the day-old chicks arrived, holidays in Kilkee and the eight-mile trudge to school. In a family with modest ambitions, and a tendency towards eccentricity, tragedy is stoically borne, troubles are endured and happiness drawn upon throughout.

ISBN 978-0-7531-9440-9 (hb)
ISBN 978-0-7531-9441-6 (pb)

A Romany in the Fields

G. Bramwell Evens

Preferring to "loiter in green meadows" discussing the balance of nature with John the Gamekeeper and learning tricks from Jerry the Poacher, Romany dons his brown tweed suit and sets off on a journey through the seasons of the countryside.

Along the way, we learn about the bravery of mother hares and how moles store worms, and watch lambs have their first taste of milk. We also see how the countryside changes from one season to another, from crisp snow to the rich colours of autumn.

ISBN 978-0-7531-9316-7 (hb)
ISBN 978-0-7531-9317-4 (pb)

Gor /B

ISIS publish a wide range of books in large print, from fiction to biography. Any suggestions for books you would like to see in large print or audio are always welcome. Please send to the Editorial Department at:

ISIS Publishing Limited
7 Centremead
Osney Mead
Oxford OX2 0ES

A full list of titles is available free of charge from:

Ulverscroft Large Print Books Limited

(UK)
The Green
Bradgate Road, Anstey
Leicester LE7 7FU
Tel: (0116) 236 4325

(Australia)
P.O. Box 314
St Leonards
NSW 1590
Tel: (02) 9436 2622

(USA)
P.O. Box 1230
West Seneca
N.Y. 14224-1230
Tel: (716) 674 4270

(Canada)
P.O. Box 80038
Burlington
Ontario L7L 6B1
Tel: (905) 637 8734

(New Zealand)
P.O. Box 456
Feilding
Tel: (06) 323 6828

Details of **ISIS** complete and unabridged audio books are also available from these offices. Alternatively, contact your local library for details of their collection of **ISIS** large print and unabridged audio books.